# The Prophecy of Oz

# The Land of Oz

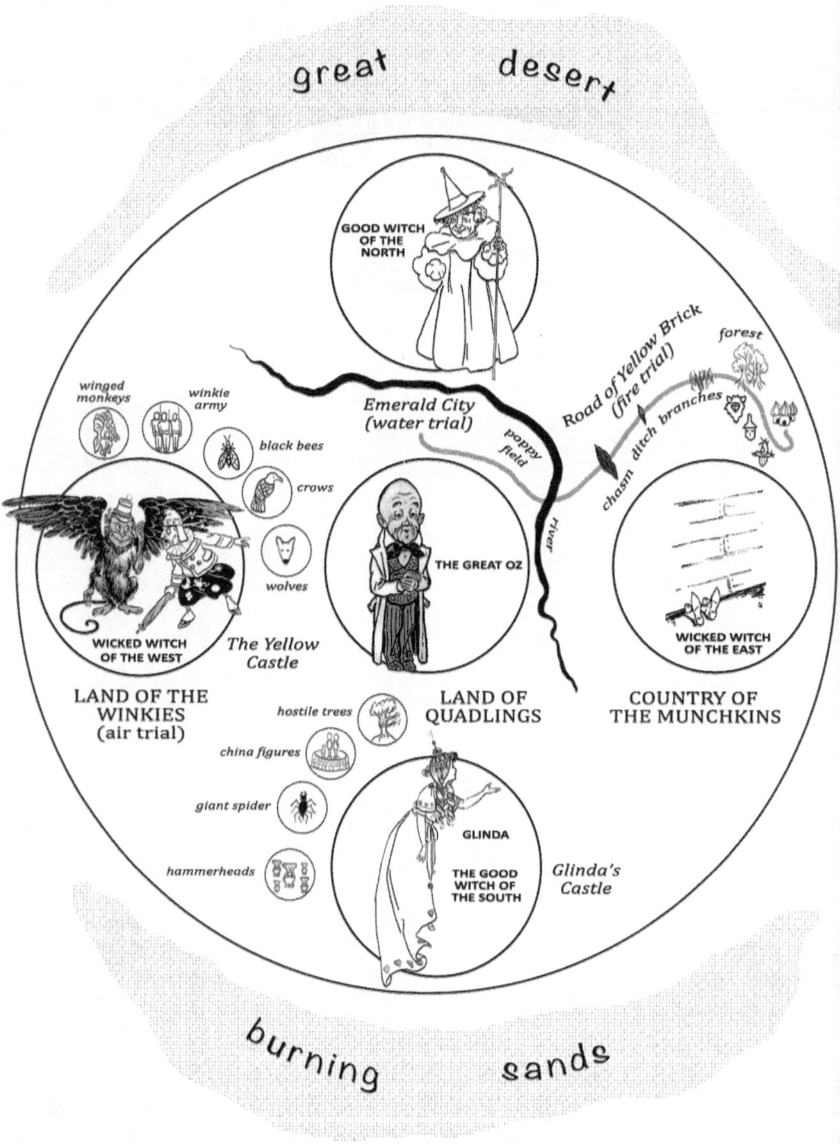

# The Prophecy of Oz

The Victory of Dorothy, the Spirit of the Americas

by Rick Spaulding

WRIGHTWOOD PRESS

ANN ARBOR

Copyright © 2017 by Rick Spaulding
All rights reserved.

Wrightwood Press
www.wrightwoodpress.org

All images except the photo of Crawford's "Freedom" are original art of W.W. Denslow published in 1900 and are in the public domain. Images have been slightly altered in color or cropped to fit the format of this book but are otherwise unchanged.
The photo of "Freedom" by Thomas Crawford was part of a series commissioned by M.C. Meigs c.1855 to document the construction of the Capitol Dome in Washington, D.C., and is in the public domain.

A digital copy of the 1900 edition of *The Wonderful Wizard of Oz* is available online from the Library of Congress:
http://www.read.gov/books/oz.html

Book design, cover design, and cover art by Maurice York. The representations of Columbia/Dorothy on the back cover are drawn from the following (clockwise): "Calliope" by Augustin Pajou, 1763 (sculpture); "Lady of Guadalupe," traditional; *America*, 1804 (engraving); "Freedom" by Thomas Crawford, 1855 (sculpture); Dorothy by William Denslow, 1899 (illustration).

NON-PROFITS, LIBRARIES, EDUCATIONAL INSTITUTIONS, WORKSHOP SPONSORS, STUDY GROUPS, ETC.
Special discounts and bulk purchases are available.
Please email sales@wrightwoodpress.org for more information.

November 2017
ISBN 978-0-9801190-6-0

# CONTENTS

| | | |
|---|---|---|
| INTRODUCTION | | 3 |
| 1. | The Cyclone and the End of American Slavery | 9 |
| 2. | The Land of the Munchkins and the End of Russian Serfdom | 14 |
| 3. | The Road of Yellow Brick and the Fire Trial | 20 |
| 4. | The City of Emeralds and the Water Trial | 29 |
| 5. | The Three Companions and the Antebellum Social Classes | 38 |
| 6. | The Wicked Witch of the West | 46 |
| 7. | The Golden Cap, Modern Plantation Slavery, and the Mexican War | 58 |
| 8. | The Attack of the Wolves and Bolshevism | 66 |
| 9. | The Attack of the Crows and Nazism | 72 |
| 10. | The Attack of the Black Bees and Americanism | 79 |
| 11. | The Winkie Army and the U.S. Army | 90 |
| 12. | The Attack of the Winged Monkeys and Terrorism | 98 |
| 13. | The Imprisonment of the Lion and the Grassroots Movement for the Rights of Undocumented Families | 105 |
| 14. | Dorothy's Victory and the Rebirth of American Culture | 109 |
| AFTERWORD | | 120 |
| REFERENCES | | |

# INTRODUCTION

Our present age is one of freedom. The attainment of this high ideal for a large number of people depends on the opportunity to obtain a decent education. The founding ideal of the United States—that all men are created equal—shone more brightly when Congress began the effort to provide American youth a universal public education in 1935. The great task entrusted to the teachers is to transmit the cultural heritage of the nation's artists and writers as well as that of the world as a whole. That heritage includes the modern counterpart of the glorious heights attained in the previous age of Ancient Greece with Homer, Sophocles and Plato. America has had its great novelists, especially Melville and Twain, its lesser-known poets—although perhaps Whitman and Dickinson will be better appreciated in the new millennium—and essayists like Emerson and Thoreau.

In the preface to *The Annotated Wizard of Oz*, Martin Gardner affirms, "Almost every great nation has its immortal work of juvenile fantasy. In England it is Lewis Carroll's *Alice* books. Germany has Grimm's fairy tales, France has the stories by Perrault, Denmark has its Andersen. Italy's classic is *Pinocchio*. In America the classic fantasy is, of course, L. Frank Baum's *The Wizard of Oz*." Just as the fantasies of other lands became an indelible part of their cultural identity, so too America's fairy tale needs to enter the thirsting souls of young Americans in a healthful way. Reading this modern fairy tale may even prove helpful to achieving the ultimate goal of Dorothy's mission: bringing the reign of the Wicked Witch of the West to an end.

In 1871 at the age of fifteen, Baum entered upon his vocation with the publication of a four-page literary paper. By 1881, he had written numerous plays and even successfully produced some of them. By the end of the 1880s, he married, and after a stint as a newspaper editor, he moved his family to Chicago in order to experience the World's Columbian Exposition of 1893. Though unable to pursue his artistic ideals in the effort to earn his daily bread and provide for his growing family, Baum yet discovered an outlet for his imagination. He excelled at storytelling, and his children—four boys—were so inquisitive about the Mother Goose rhymes he was reading to them that he began to make up stories to answer their questions. During one of these elaborate inventions, his wife, Maud, overheard him and urged him to write it down. Her advice turned out to be the best he would ever receive and resulted in a children's book, *Mother Goose in Prose*, published in 1897.

Fortune continued to smile on him, and the following year he met William Denslow. Like L. Frank Baum, Denslow had been attracted by the upcoming Columbian Exposition and had moved to Chicago. A noted artist, he had joined the

Chicago Press Club, which was composed of Chicago's most important writers and artists. When Baum became a member in 1898, the two men formed a partnership to publish a small book of Baum's poems. They worked together on the various children's verses of Baum and called it, *Father Goose, His Book*. The combination of beautiful illustrations and a writing style like that of Lewis Carroll produced a unique children's book and a stunning success. It sold out immediately, as did several subsequent editions. The book established its forty-three-year-old author as the foremost children's writer in America.

Baum and Denslow quickly turned to a new project, even more ambitious, a "modernized fairy tale." The story of how *The Wonderful Wizard of Oz* came to be is best told by Baum himself: "I was sitting on the hat rack in the hall, telling the kids a story and suddenly this one moved right in and took possession. I shooed the children away and grabbed a piece of paper that was lying there on the rack and began to write. It really seemed to write itself. Then I couldn't find any regular paper, so I took anything at all, even a bunch of old envelopes." When Baum eventually finished the work on October 9, 1899, he knew how special it was. He took a piece of paper, inscribed upon it, "With this pencil I wrote the manuscript of 'The Emerald City,'" and dated it. He attached the stub of the pencil to the paper, framed it, and hung it over his writing desk.

The reading public immediately embraced Baum's fairy tale, quickly buying out the first edition and countless printings that followed. The Wonderful Wizard of Oz was not only America's first fairy tale, but over a hundred years later, it remains its most beloved. Following on the heels of its immense popularity, literary critics showed an increasing interest in Baum's fairy tale, and sought to uncover what allegorical, psychological or sociological motifs might have so captured the American imagination. Some critics focused on the archetypal nature of Baum's characters and sought universal meaning in them. An important attempt in this direction came from an English professor at the University of Georgia, John Algeo, who presented a theosophical interpretation of the tale. It was an appropriate viewpoint for a professor who would later become the president of the Theosophical Society, a group that Baum himself had joined in 1892. The land of Oz, from Algeo's point of view, was a "mandala," a geometric flat land characterized by its four cardinal directions. In this soul world dwelt the archetypes of the human soul, the three companions whom Dorothy befriended. Algeo called them thinking, feeling, and willing and pointed out the virtues that the three soul forces strove to attain: strong intellect, dauntless courage, and spotless purity. He highlighted the theme of self-development as he traced Dorothy's journey down the road of yellow brick, the symbol of the path of initiation. Her goal was the Emerald City, where she would find her teacher or guru.

While Algeo was especially interested in the universal significance of Baum's characters, other critics looked to the tumultuous social forces of Baum's day and discovered a resonance with actual events rather than archetypal motifs. Henry Littlefield first proposed the idea that the incidents of the journey of Dorothy and her three companions represented historical occurrences in America and a prophecy of America's future. His view of Baum's fairy tale as a parable on Populism has been discredited, but his attempt to understand Dorothy's companions in relation to the social classes of America resonated with early philosophical traditions that sought to understand the soul forces by exploring how they manifest in societal forms that people have created for themselves. The first major work of philosophy, Plato's *Republic*, took this very approach by revealing the activity of the three soul forces in the macrocosm of the social organism before drawing a parallel to the inner life by identifying their activity in the microcosm of the human being.

Littlefield presented his interpretation in 1964 and compared the characters to the social groups and the Populist movement active at the time Baum wrote his tale.[1] He viewed the Scarecrow as the farmers, the Tin Woodman as Eastern labor, and the Cowardly Lion as William Jennings Bryan, the leader of the Populist movement. Littlefield cited Baum's experiences in South Dakota as the basis for his use of the Scarecrow as a symbol of the Midwestern farmer. The element of volition—called by Plato the appetitive soul—Littlefield saw manifest in the Tin Woodman, whose work had been dehumanized by Eastern witchcraft as he had become a kind of machine-man made all of tin. Littlefield proposed that Baum pictured the plight of the worker in the Eastern factories, overworked and laid off by periodic depressions, in the Tin Woodman's paralyzed state and his feeling that he had lost all human emotions. Between Eastern industrial workers and the Western farmer stood the common man—the Lion.

Littlefield pointed to the powerful speeches of Bryan, which Baum had heard in the torchlight parades of 1896, as the basis for Baum's use of the Cowardly Lion as a symbol of the Populist movement.

Littlefield also suggested that Dorothy is Baum's Miss Everyman. His view contrasts most remarkably with Algeo's theosophical interpretation, which concluded that Dorothy was simply a soul seeking to leave the cycle of death and rebirth and return to Nirvana. Like-minded critics went so far as to expand of Littlefield's view of Dorothy by calling her Uncle Sam, suggesting a second insight to be gleaned from Littlefield's work: that the social classes of America are ruled over by a powerful folk soul that embodies the nation's ideals.

Baum's allegory, according to Littlefield, is that the Silver Shoes worn by Dorothy stand for the silver standard and the road of yellow brick for the gold standard. At the time of Baum's writing, American currency was officially backed by gold. Dorothy's journey with her three friends to the Emerald City, according to the Populist interpretation, shows that Baum envisioned a solution to America's ills by adopting silver as backing for the American dollar in addition to the gold reserves then in use. Here the Populist view begins to break down, as the advice of the good Witch of the North to follow the road of yellow brick becomes twisted into an allegory about Bryan becoming President. Chapter 5 of this book presents an effort to correct this misinterpretation.

# Chapter 1

## THE CYCLONE AND THE END OF AMERICAN SLAVERY

As Baum opens his tale, Dorothy is living in a house on the Kansas prairie:

When Dorothy stood in the doorway and looked around, she could see nothing but the great gray prairie on every side. Not a tree nor a house broke the broad sweep of flat country that reached the edge of the sky in all directions. The sun had baked the plowed land into a gray mass, with little cracks running through it. Even the grass was not green, for the sun had burned the tops of the long blades until they were the same gray color to be seen everywhere.

When Aunt Em came there to live she was a young, pretty wife. The sun and wind had changed her, too. They had taken the sparkle from her eyes and left them a sober gray; they had taken the red from her cheeks and lips, and they were gray also. She was thin and gaunt, and never smiled now. When Dorothy, who was an orphan, first came to her, Aunt Em had been so startled by the child's laughter that she would scream and press her hand upon her heart whenever Dorothy's merry voice reached her ears; and she still looked at the little girl with wonder that she could find anything to laugh at.

Uncle Henry never laughed. He worked hard from morning till night and did not know what joy was. He was gray also, from his long beard to his rough boots, and he looked stern and solemn, and rarely spoke.

It was Toto that made Dorothy laugh, and saved her from growing as gray as her other surroundings. Toto was not gray; he was a little black dog, with long silky hair and small black eyes that twinkled merrily on either side of his funny, wee nose. Toto played all day long, and Dorothy played with him, and loved him dearly.

If Baum's description of Kansas and its people were to be connected to historical events, then historians would likely relate it to the Dust Bowl and the ravages of the Great Depression on Midwestern farms. Yet Baum wrote his story in 1899, a full thirty years before these twin disasters destroyed the heartland for a generation. Tempting though it may be to find an easy parallel to the grayness of Kansas, the uniformity of drained color suggests something more mysterious at work since the graying land is reflected in the similarly graying people. Both served as an amazing backdrop for the miraculous young heroine and her magical dog, Toto.

The opening description of the aging forces active in the Kansas landscape gives way to the first event of the plot:

> From the far north they heard a low wail of the wind, and Uncle Henry and Dorothy could see where the long grass bowed in waves before the coming storm. There now came a sharp whistling in

the air from the south, and as they turned their eyes that way they saw ripples in the grass coming from that direction also.

Suddenly Uncle Henry stood up.

'There's a cyclone coming, Em,' he called to his wife; 'I'll go look after the stock.'²

This coming together of a storm front from the north and another from the south has a specific meaning if it is viewed spiritually. Rudolf Steiner presented a description of such an event in relation to experiences in the third region of the country of spiritual beings in his book *Theosophy*. "Here, for example, we can talk about thunderstorms with flashing lightning and rolling thunder; if we pursue the matter further, we find that these spiritual storms express the passions of battles being fought."³ Historians would likely identify a battle occurring in Kansas during the nineteenth century as the event of "Bleeding Kansas," the consequence of the South's attempt to overturn the Missouri Compromise with the passage of the Kansas-Nebraska Act in 1854. The storm fronts coming from the north and the south may show what lived in the souls of the American people during this event. Baum's picture of Dorothy being swept away may suggest that the rulership of the Spirit of America ended due to the confusion and rage that seethed within the souls of the people of both the North and the South. The cyclone may thus picture that event in American history called the Civil War. As the house containing Dorothy lifted off the ground and carried her away, a kind of echo of Lincoln's warning to the American people may be heard: "A house divided against itself cannot stand."

Dorothy, as the folk soul of America, certainly occupied a foremost place in the collective aspirations and imaginations of her country. Columbia, as the Founding Fathers named her, was ever-present in popular music, in art and sculpture, and even on the coinage of the United States for well over a century. The national song was "Hail! Columbia," a catchy tune written in 1799 that remained the anthem until 1933. The original name of the nation's capital was "Washington, in the Territory of Columbia"—changed through the generations to "District of Columbia" and today simply abbreviated as "D.C." What then is the meaning of Dorothy being torn away from her role as the guiding spirit of the American people by this great cyclone of the Civil War? A hint to the answer of this question can be found in the poetry of Walt Whitman, who considered himself to be the mouthpiece of his country's guiding spirit, whom he variously called Libertad, Democracy, Columbia, and Mother. In "By Blue Ontario's Shore," published in 1866 just after the conclusion of the war to end slavery, Whitman narrated a vision in which he told how the Civil War had changed Columbia and how, since the war's end, she had withdrawn from the nation and had become accessible only to those individuals who seek her out of their own freedom and inner resolve. Both Baum and Denslow came to Chicago to see the Columbian Exposition, the world's fair dedicated to Columbia, whose sixty-six-foot-high statue was designed by Daniel French. Called "The Republic," it was the centerpiece of the White City on the shores of Lake Michigan.

The reason for this strange state of affairs regarding the lack of knowledge of Columbia as the folk soul of America has to do with the nature of freedom and liberty itself. Only the actual living activity of thinking can gain access to Columbia. One's own intuition is always the starting point of a free deed, but each additional step on the path requires an equally deep enlivening and ensouling process that allows the idea to live and grow. Active thinking allows thoughts to grow organically. Only such living thoughts can express truth and avoid the emptiness of intellections, those abstract, shadowy, dead thoughts in their final form. The war to end slavery may have compelled the very being of liberty itself to leave her people so that she would not interfere with their freedom. The American people can still experience her guidance and blessings, but only if they make the necessary inner effort.

# Chapter 2
# THE LAND OF THE MUNCHKINS
## AND THE END OF RUSSIAN SERFDOM

The cyclone gently deposited Dorothy in the east of the Land of Oz, in Munchkin land. If Dorothy represents the American nation spirit, one might expect that she would have landed in the West, in the Country of the Winkies. The description of the Land of Oz that Dorothy heard upon her arrival in Munchkinland indicated to Algeo that the Land of Oz was a mandala of the whole soul world, the astral counterpart of the whole earthly realm, a flat land of imagination corresponding geographically to the physical plane. Following the pattern of the mandala, Kansas, representing America, would find its astral or soul complement in the western Country of the Winkies. Instead, Dorothy's lengthy journey carried her to a land of imagination apparently complementary to Russia. Her later visit to the home of a well-to-do Munchkin farmer introduced her to a kindly man, hospitable and sincere. The compassion of the Munchkins points to a character trait of the Russian people that the novelist Leo Tolstoy found in the Russian peasants, a way of life that he devoted himself to in his last days. The Munchkin homes, with their circular shape and domes, seem to indicate not just a physical residence, but the soul counterpart of the Russian Orthodox churches where the people worshipped. The color that the Munchkins loved, blue, conveys a feeling of reverence and restful quiet. Their slight stature suggests that their activity in Munchkin land includes only a part of the human soul, that part which journeys to the land of dreams during sleep.

Dorothy's arrival in the blue land of the Munchkins was the second event of the plot. It proved to be as monumentally important as the first since the falling house crushed and killed the wicked Witch of the East. When told that she had killed the Eastern Witch, Dorothy protested that she didn't mean to and that it wasn't her fault, lending a comic twist to the plot device of serendipity. Her happy accident offset America's loss of its national spirit, as it were, as though the ill wind of the cyclone had blown somebody some good.

The Witch of the East is certainly wicked. She is connected with the ancient spirituality of the East, though held back and preserved in a horribly twisted manner. She is a picture of spirituality become decadent. While serfdom did have a proper role to play in the development of the Middle Ages and feudalism, its preservation in Russia in modern times resulted in the perpetual indenture of the peasant class and formed the basis for the power and wealth of the Russian czars and nobility. The end of serfdom in 1861 seemed to come out of the blue, and historians to this day have presented little explanation for the decree of Czar Alexander II that freed the serfs—some twenty-three million in number—from slavery. The serfs rejoiced, perhaps even more so due to the unexpectedness of their freedom. The joy that the Russian peasants felt seems to manifest in the Munchkins' celebration—a harbinger of the celebration that the Winkies will later hold in Dorothy's honor.

The situation in Russia at the time of the American Civil War was the outcome of the policies of rulers like Ivan the Terrible and reformers like Peter the Great. Whatever else historians might want to say about such czars, the Russian peasants recognized them in a way that accords with the picture Baum presents, as instruments of the dark power of the wicked Witch of the East. There was no civil war in Russia to end serfdom, though certainly there was discontent enough for one. Instead, an inspiration of a progressive, positive kind seems to have enlightened Czar Alexander II. How could the Russian czar have decided to end serfdom and turn away from that influence that had ruled Russia since the time of the Mongol invasion? Certainly historians must use the documents in their possession to come up with their own answers, but the picture that Baum provides also lends insight. The house falling out of the sky shows a kind of spiritual cause-and-effect that allows the reader a glimpse into the world of providence. In her most famous pose, Columbia/Dorothy, as the Statue of Liberty, holds a torch aloft to the world, a beacon of freedom. If a spirit of this significance to all nations should be displaced from her rightful home, then it makes sense that just such a spirit would bring about good wherever she might land. The fact that Baum presents the death of the wicked Witch of the East as an accident pictures this serendipitous event as part of the divine plan, and in some way a prefiguring of Dorothy's youthful inexperience and ignorance of her own power.

The Munchkins seemed to sense the importance of this event, accident or no, and they celebrated. They could not believe their good fortune and gave all the credit to Dorothy. Whereas in Kansas Dorothy was isolated and alone, now she is surrounded by little people. This picture points to the meaning of Dorothy's departure from the earthly plane of existence and her arrival in the soul world. On the earthly plane, the living souls of the American people were invisible to her and only revealed themselves as a storm, the great tornado that carried Dorothy away. In the soul world, the individual souls of human beings now become visible to her.

Chapter Two introduces a new main character, the good Witch of the North, who takes on the role of spirit guide to Dorothy. She is the counterpart of Glinda, the Good Witch of the South, and rules over the first third of the book just as Glinda does the last third. The idea of a spirit guide implies a path of initiation, which results from the efforts of full initiates who open the way so that earnest students may follow and have some hope for success. The middle third of the book is ruled over by the Great Oz, who also gives his name to the book as a whole. The mission that the good Witch of the North now gives to Dorothy—to go to the City of Emeralds—seems indisputably less important than the one that the Wizard will later give her, the task of destroying the Wicked Witch of the West. The truth is that they are interdependent. Advancing on the road of yellow brick—the path of self-development, or the initiate's path—is necessary in order to properly face the Wicked Witch. Without insight into oneself and the development of one's own soul forces, gained through personal struggle and development of virtue, resistance to evil forces such as the Witches would be inadequate and feeble. Despite her early success with the wicked Witch of the East, Dorothy's opposition to the much more powerful Wicked Witch of the West can be no accident; it must be conscious and deliberate.

The full range of knowledge that the good Witch of the North possessed helped Dorothy in many concrete ways. The Good Witch put her cap on the tip of her nose, and it became a slate. Writing appeared and gave Dorothy beneficent guidance, namely, to go to the Emerald City—the original title of Baum's fairy tale. The Good Witch advised Dorothy to follow the road of yellow brick. She also told Dorothy that the Silver Shoes were hers. She didn't tell her what their power was. A spirit guide cannot reveal what the spirit pupil must learn for herself.

Though the Silver Shoes belonged to the wicked Witch of the East, they were not evil. Dorothy did not suspect their power; only at the end of her journey will she be told of their full import. The Silver Shoes are one of the most significant pictures that Baum presents. Their color points to the moon. Gaining control of the moon forces will eventually enable Dorothy to return to the earthly plane of existence. Mythology pictures a similar power in the winged sandals of Mercury. The messenger of the gods possesses the power to travel between the realm of Olympus and that of mortal man. The power of the Silver Shoes is greater than that of the winged sandals. They permit their bearer to enter fully into the earthly realm and to remain there. At this point in the story Dorothy simply accepts the great gift given to her and exhibits surprise at how perfectly they fit, and how helpful they prove to be on her journey.

The parting kiss that the good Witch of the North gave to Dorothy provided her with more immediately practical help. Protection such as a spirit guide can offer is not generally something of which the student is immediately aware. Dorothy, like many spirit pupils, only gradually comes to appreciate the protection that such a kiss bestows: the blessing that no one would dare injure a person who has been kissed by the good Witch of the North.

# Chapter 3

# THE ROAD OF YELLOW BRICK
### and the Fire Trial

---

After washing up and putting some food in a basket, Dorothy decided to change out of her old, worn-out leather shoes and into her new Silver Shoes, which coincidentally fit her feet perfectly. She and Toto then set forth on their journey to the Emerald City, finding the road of yellow brick with little difficulty. Dorothy met the Scarecrow first, stuck on a pole in the middle of a cornfield. Dorothy easily lifted him off the pole since he was made of straw. The Scarecrow announced that he felt like "a new man" and expressed his gratitude. He inquired with great curiosity about Dorothy, the Emerald City, and Kansas. Talkative and friendly, he was also willing to confide in Dorothy and tell her that he felt himself to be a fool, as a crow had once called him. He joined Dorothy on her quest to see the Wizard in the hope of receiving "brains" from him.

The Scarecrow represents the soul force of thinking. Though his greatest desire is to receive the gift of brains, he is far from stupid, as he will show in the trials to come. He seems to possess a certain common sense that he will use to advise and assist Dorothy, unable as he is to accomplish any action or deed other than merely walking. The archetypal symbol of thinking is the eagle, pictured by the constellation of Aquila. While the common sense of the Scarecrow certainly has its feet on the ground, the straw that fills his head bears a certain resemblance to the hollow bones of birds. Even the purpose of the Scarecrow points to his kinship with feathered creatures—his job is to scare away crows. The thinking of the newly-made Scarecrow pictures the thoughts of modern man, of the consciousness soul, the soul force whose activity has only recently appeared in history. Not living, organic thoughts, but intellections, as Ralph Waldo Emerson called them—earthbound abstractions that mirror the hollowness of straw—are the characteristic thoughts of the present day. Not just the Scarecrow has bemoaned such thinking, but poets as well. T. S. Eliot is quite clear about the problem in his poem "The Hollow Men":

> We are the hollow men
> We are the stuffed men
> Leaning together
> Headpiece filled with straw. Alas!
> Our dried voices, when
> We whisper together
> Are quiet and meaningless
> As wind in dry grass
> Or rats' feet over broken glass
> In our dry cellar

The shame that the Scarecrow felt from self-awareness of his situation led him to call himself a fool. Nor did his helpful suggestions on the journey down the road of yellow brick serve to change this opinion of himself, which derived from his failure to scare away the crows. Thrice more he would call himself a fool, the last after his visit to the throne room in the Palace of Oz. The archetypal symbol of the fool is the goose. The hero of Wolfram von Eschenbach's medieval epic, *Parzival*, began his adventures as the fool, the embodiment of the problem of modern thinking, who takes words too literally, fails to appreciate their context and deeper meaning, and mistakes the letter of the word for its spirit. The hollowness of the fool's thoughts points to the deep need in the present age to enliven thoughts that have become parched and dry, alienated from the living world they should represent.

After staying the night in a cottage near the road, Dorothy met her second companion, the Tin Woodman, in a forest. He was rusted in place, and his joints needed lubrication for him to work properly again. He is the polar opposite of Dorothy's first companion, the Scarecrow. The Woodman is heavy and made of tin, whereas the Scarecrow is light and filled with straw. The story of his life stretches far back in time to when he was actually a human being, before being dismembered and reconstructed piece by piece into the Tin Woodman. The Scarecrow, by contrast, is newly-made. The Tin Woodman's foremost characteristic is his kindness. He also carries an axe, which proves very useful on the journey down the road of yellow brick. His purposeful activity stands in stark contrast to the Scarecrow's lack of deeds.

Literary critics tend to view the Tin Woodman as a symbol of the feeling realm, the emotions, or what Plato called the "enspirited soul." Their view ignores his ever-present axe and mechanical parts and contradicts Littlefield's insight into his connection to the working class and the modern phenomenon of the alienation of labor—the soul-less, mechanistic nature of factory jobs that place the laborer in danger of losing his heart forces. The contrast of the Tin Woodman and the Scarecrow suggests the polarity of willing and thinking in the human soul, and offers an interpretation more in line with Baum's characterization. The archetypal symbol of the force of willing or volition is the bull. Egyptian astrology places the Bull (Taurus) opposite to the Scorpion, pointing to the fallen nature of thinking. The Tin Woodman's life story may refer to this bygone era when the sentient soul (the appetitive soul, or the force of volition) began its development.

The desire of the Tin Woodman to have a heart is the reason many critics identify him as the force of feeling. His love for a Munchkin girl led to his tragic fate. His true character, symbolized by the axe, was turned against him by the magic enchantment of the wicked Witch of the East. The Tin Woodman's loss of his heart is similar to the myths of the dismemberment of Osiris or Dionysius. The absence of a heart ironically underscores the actual difficulty that the Tin Woodman must surmount, a tendency to sentimentality so great that stepping on a beetle causes him to weep until he rusts and becomes incapacitated and paralyzed as when Dorothy first found him. His internal obstacle mirrors that of the Scarecrow. Each struggles with a feeling of hollowness that shapes their personalities into the Sentimentalist and the Fool. The Tin Woodman, the soul force of willing, needs a heart and the feelings of human love to function properly. The Scarecrow, to avoid being a fool, must overcome intellectual thinking and enliven his thoughts to find real solutions to life's dilemmas.

The third companion, the Cowardly Lion, came to Dorothy out of a great forest that surrounded the road of yellow brick. The Lion attacked the Scarecrow and the Tin Woodman and was going to eat Toto when Dorothy ran up and slapped him on the face. The slap served to stop the Lion's attack, revealing him to be a bully and a coward. The Lion is the archetypal symbol of the feeling realm, the enspirited soul, which Plato identifies with the virtue of courage. The Lion and Dorothy form a polarity, as do the Scarecrow and the Tin Woodman. It is Dorothy who stops the Lion in her defense of Toto. The Cowardly Lion stands in opposition to the polarity of the Scarecrow and the Tin Woodman. He, like Dorothy, is a "meat" character, while they are "artificial" ones. He is horizontal, while they stand vertically. All three representatives of the soul forces experience a form of hollowness. The Lion's is internal, while that of the other two is external. The three soul forces willingly joined Dorothy on the road of yellow brick in the hope of mending the deficiencies that beset them. Dorothy provided a higher purpose to their journey, uniting them in their ostensive task of self-development.

The journey of Dorothy and her three companions down the road of yellow brick has not proved especially fertile for those literary critics who have attempted to explore its historical meaning. Their critiques have included numerous contradictions, a one-sided view of Baum's politics, and stretched allegorical interpretations, perhaps owing to their insistence on finding direct parallels to American history. By contrast, Baum's other critics, looking for a personal meaning, have found the journey ideally suited to their purposes, since the very idea of a path of initiation involves a spiritual guide. The good Witch of the North appears to Dorothy as just such a guide. She recommends that Dorothy take the road of yellow brick and demonstrates her humility, selflessness, and kindness through the gift of the Silver Shoes, her advice, and her kiss. These deeds give Dorothy the means, the clear path, and the protection that a good spirit guide would provide her pupil. The destination at the end of the road further emphasizes the possibility that Dorothy's journey is a path of initiation. The Emerald City and the Great Wizard residing there suggest a spiritual temple with a leader therein who can assist the three companions with their task of self-development and provide the wanderer a way home.

That Dorothy meets her companions upon the road of yellow brick is the most important reason to view it as a path of initiation. Critics like Algeo, who are familiar with the esoteric paths of initiation as found in theosophy or the spiritual paths implicit within the various religions of the world, cannot help but connect Dorothy's three companions with the three soul forces of thinking, feeling, and willing. Taking up the path of initiation begins with insight into one's own soul and the decision of the self, or ego, to attempt to purify it. The very desire of the Scarecrow, the Tin Woodman, and the Cowardly Lion to overcome their weaknesses resonate with the words found over the portal to Apollo's oracle at Delphi to "Know thyself"—to undertake the transformation of one's own soul. The Scarecrow, the friendly and curious representative of human thinking, possessed common sense but lacked confidence and suffered from the very newness of his earthly activity. The Tin Woodman, the kindly and sentimental symbol of volition, promised the possibility of industrious activity but tended to paralysis due to his complete reshaping during his lengthy earthly sojourn. Lastly, the Lion, the archetypal symbol of the emotive life, felt himself to be a coward and in need of what he once had had—courage.

The first tests on the road of yellow brick involved the three companions, each in turn. After freeing the Scarecrow, Dorothy came to a great forest that obscured the road. Using common sense, the Scarecrow suggested continuing the journey despite the darkness. On the path of initiation the way forward may not seem clear and its future direction may be uncertain, but a common sense approach is necessary. Dorothy followed the good advice of the Scarecrow and passed the test of thinking. After oiling the Tin Woodman and having him join their journey, Dorothy came to a part of the road obstructed by branches. The Tin Woodman said that he could solve their problem with his axe, which he did. The path of initiation may be beset with obstacles, and the pupil may face difficulties that hinder further progress. This test of willing requires actions that remove the hindrances, that cut through the problems that block passage. Dorothy found that her oiling of the Tin Woodman's joints now paid a handsome dividend since he could remove the obstructing branches. When a ditch created a break in the road and threatened to halt their journey entirely, the Cowardly Lion decided that he could leap over it. Gathering his courage, he did so, not once, but five times in all, proving his mettle and bringing all the members of the party to the other side. A situation may arise such that the future course of the path of initiation is obvious and apparent, but the way to it may not be so. The path of initiation at this point may require something like a leap of faith. The test of feeling demonstrates that sufficient courage exists in the soul to continue the journey. The wanderer must complete these initial tests of the three soul forces in order to proceed. Dorothy and her companions face obstacles that characterize this phase of self-development: when darkness, obstructions, or disruption confront the spirit pupil on the path of initiation, then common sense, perseverance, and courage must come to the fore.

The fourth test on the road of yellow brick began when Dorothy and her companions found a yawning chasm much wider than the ditch the Lion had leapt over, which halted any further progress. The Scarecrow suggested cutting down a nearby tree so that it would fall over the abyss and form a bridge. The Tin Woodman obliged with his axe, and the Cowardly Lion pushed the tree to help it fall in the right direction. No sooner had they executed this part of the plan than a more pressing problem arose, one that the Lion had warned of earlier. Two Kalidahs appeared, and the monstrous, ferocious beasts began running toward Dorothy and her companions. The roar of the Lion stopped them, but only temporarily. The

Scarecrow suggested crossing to the other side of the chasm. Once there, he advised cutting down the tree-bridge so that the Kalidahs couldn't follow them. The Tin Woodman completed the task just as the beasts were attempting to cross over, and they fell into the pit below.

The fourth test required the concerted efforts of all three soul forces and constituted the first great trial on the path of initiation. Constructing a bridge in order to continue following the path points to the quality of initiative that is necessary at this juncture. If the soul force of thinking possesses this trait, then the other soul forces can work in harmony with it and create the needed pathway. An element of danger is also present, and it has led to this ordeal being called the "fire trial." The Kalidahs, monstrous beasts with bodies like bears, heads like tigers, and horribly sharp claws, were already known to the Lion, the representative of the feeling life. They are the sensual desires that rise up and threaten to overwhelm the soul that cannot recognize their danger and avoid their ravages. The Scarecrow again played the leading role and created a plan to protect the soul and spirit. The importance that thinking plays in the fire trial has led this trial to be called the "trial of common sense."

# Chapter 4
# THE CITY OF EMERALDS
### AND THE WATER TRIAL

After passing the first ordeal of the soul, the fire trial, Dorothy and her companions arrived at a broad river. The Scarecrow, again employing his common sense, asked the Tin Woodman to build the company a raft. The Tin Woodman completed the task, and the company boarded the raft and pushed off from the shore using poles. Once they reached the middle of the river, the strong current there threatened to sweep them downstream to the Country of the Winkies. The depth of the river meant that the poles were useless. When the Scarecrow's pole finally struck again, he pushed so hard it got stuck in the river bottom. Hanging on to it, he was pulled from the raft and left behind. The courage of the Lion saved the remaining company. He decided to swim for shore and asked the Tin Woodman to grab hold of his tail so that the raft would follow him. Arriving on shore, they started the long walk back to the road of yellow brick. Dorothy met a Stork near where the Scarecrow had been abandoned and asked him for help. The Stork flew to the Scarecrow, lifted him off his pole, and returned him to the company.

This second great trial of the soul has traditionally been called the "water trial." The motif of the trials of the soul appears in many great works of Western culture. Mozart included both the fire trial and the water trial in his opera, *The Magic Flute*, which he completed just before his death in 1791. Baum's presentation of the water trial begins appropriately with the test of crossing a river. While common sense has served admirably up to this point, it can no longer play the primary part in the soul's drama. The representative of the feeling life has to step bravely forward and accomplish the first test posed by the water trial. Skipping over this stage of soul development and journeying downstream would mean facing the threat of the Wicked Witch of the West before the faculties of the soul, in their weakened condition, were up to such a task. The Cowardly Lion, carrying out his mission without the firm support of dry land, swam his way across and united Dorothy and the three companions once again. The earth-bound thinking of the Scarecrow received assistance from the Stork, who is a symbol of the creative thinking that can appear at this stage of self-development.

After the detour down the river, the attempt to return to the road of yellow brick took Dorothy and her companions through a poppy field. Dorothy felt her eyes grow heavy, and she wished to sit down and rest. The Tin Woodman and the Scarecrow encouraged her to keep walking, but soon Dorothy could stand no longer and fell asleep amidst the beautiful red poppies. The Cowardly Lion also mentioned how tired he was. The Scarecrow advised the Lion to run out of the field of poppies, which, he surmised, was sending the "meat characters" into a deep sleep. The Lion obeyed with what strength he had left. The Scarecrow, with the help of the Tin Woodman, then devised a means of carrying Dorothy and Toto away from the fragrant, narcotic fumes of the poppy. They lifted the sleeping Dorothy and Toto and transported them out of the meadow. Near the meadow's edge they saw the sleeping Lion, who had to be left behind. While waiting for Dorothy to awaken, the Tin Woodman saw a fierce Wildcat chasing a mouse. He was struck by the injustice of it and pitied the poor mouse. As the Wildcat ran past, the Tin Woodman's axe swept down and ended the Wildcat's life, saving the mouse. The mouse then came up to the Tin Woodman and thanked him, informing him that she was the Queen of the field mice and would repay him for saving her life. The Scarecrow intervened at this point and concocted a plan that sent the Tin Woodman off to build a large cart, and the mice to find long pieces of string. Together they managed to get the Lion on the cart and pull him out of the meadow.

The poppy field was the second test of the water trial, which Dorothy and her companions had to pass through before they were ready to enter the Emerald City. The Scarecrow, who had lost his leadership role to the Lion during the river crossing, now came to his aid when the great beast fell prey to the allure of the poppy's fumes. The Scarecrow's creative plan, however, depended on the good deed of the Tin Woodman and another strange and wonderful creature. The Queen of the field mice indicates a development of the feeling life similar to that of the creative thinking symbolized by the Stork. When the Tin Woodman's axe ended the savage assault of the Wildcat—a picture of untamed feelings similar to the Kalidahs during the fire trial—the shy creature of the field demonstrated her devotion and that of her followers. The field mice joined their strings to the cart bearing the sleeping Lion, and they pulled with thousands of tiny tugs. The field mice—in ancient Greece sacred to the god of Delphi and a symbol of reverence—hint at the change in feeling that should occur at this stage of the soul's development. The Queen also gave Dorothy a gift, a whistle—a manifest symbol of this mood of devotion—that will allow her to call the mice to her whenever needed.

After completing the test of the poppy field, the journey down the road of yellow brick proved uneventful. The Land of Oz was different from the Country of the Munchkins in another way as well. The color of the whole land and everything in it was green, not blue, as the travelers soon noticed. It was located in the center of the greater mandala of Oz. Its color may suggest the role of this land as mediator between the blue of the Eastern lands and the yellow of the West. When the company arrived at the Emerald City, they met the Guardian of the Gate, who warned them not to seek entrance if they lacked honesty or came out of idle curiosity. These warnings suggest that passing the tests of the road of yellow brick should lead to a corresponding development of character in order to proceed further. The sincere desire of the three companions to mend the weaknesses inherent in each of them, and Dorothy's hope to gain knowledge of how to return to Kansas, showed their request for entry was neither dishonest nor idle.

The Guardian then attached spectacles to each member of the company. In order to enter the city, the companions had to adopt a new way of seeing. The fact that all citizens of the city were required to wear the same glasses suggests that a different form of consciousness reigned therein. In ordinary life spectacles or eyeglasses are used to see the world more clearly. For near-sighted and far-sighted people, glasses bring the objects of the world into sharper focus. They enable people to see three-dimensional objects more distinctly. The pupil who undertakes the arduous task of self-development often falls victim to illusion by bringing this idea of physical sight into the imaginative world—into the soul world—and by expecting this world to behave in the same way as the world of everyday consciousness. Insofar as the pupil attempts to view living imaginations as if through spectacles that can bring them like solid objects into sharper focus, he or she hallucinates. The spirit pupil who carries over the earthly way of seeing into the soul world sees figments of the imagination, not living thoughts. Only gradually does the pupil learn to live with such imaginations, enter into them, and become one with them. The eye of imagination is not a camera as is the physical eye; rather it is a soul organ that sheds light on what it illumines and unites with what it sees. In terms of philosophy, one could say that Imaginative consciousness represents the overcoming of the subject-object dichotomy. Baum's picture of the spectacles suggests that taking such a step in knowledge is easier said than done.

A feeling of awe gradually descended on Dorothy and her companions as they walked through the Emerald City. The streets and houses seemed to be constructed of green marble studded everywhere with sparkling emeralds. The people seemed happy, contented, and prosperous. Strangely, there seemed to be no animals, not even a horse, and certainly no lions. The children of the city actually hid when they saw the Lion. Part of the explanation for the order and harmony in the Emerald City has to do with the Great Oz, the ruler. He had not enslaved his people as the evil witches had done to the Munchkins and the Winkies. When Dorothy and her companions spent a night at a farmhouse outside of the city, they discovered that the citizens of the Land of Oz were well aware of the gifts that their ruler had at his command. The farmer had assured the travelers that the Great Oz possessed a pot of courage, a collection of hearts, and more brains than he knew what to do with. The citizens of the Land of Oz were thus familiar with the basic task of self-development: the harmonization of the three soul forces. The description of the people emphasizes their attainment of virtues in their emotive life (happy), their thinking (contented), and their life of volition (prosperous). The Great Oz may have confounded the people of his realm with his refusal to give audiences and his demand that they wear spectacles, but he had clearly assisted them on the path of initiation. The glory of the Emerald City demonstrated the advance in self-knowledge that the good Wizard had fostered. The lack of animals may indicate the ascendancy of human reason within this realm.

The Palace of Oz was the goal of Dorothy's first mission, the one given to her by the good Witch of the North. The journey down the road of yellow brick had led her to the mystery temple, the culmination of the path of initiation. Unlike the Grail Castle in Eschenbach's *Parzival*, which was sheltered by impenetrable woods and thickets, this temple stood in the exact center of a city. The Guardian of the Gate seemed to be tasked with protecting those who sought entrance to the palace, rather than guarding the palace itself. The ostensive reason for the spectacles was that the brightness of the Emerald City would blind the visitor were they not worn. Thus does the palace resemble the destination in Plato's *Republic*, which the initiate could only attain by leaving the cave and gradually became accustomed to the glory of the spirit sun, the Idea of the Good. The Neoplatonists, who further developed the ideas of the founder of philosophy, called Plato's path of initiation the Royal Road and its high purpose the encounter with the Logos. The color of the road of yellow brick points to the idea that it represents the sun road, the path of philosophy to the sun temple. While the Great Oz is not the Logos, he did help shape his palace into a replica of the true sun temple, organized life in the Emerald City to reflect wisdom, and aided the progress of reason in the Land of Oz.

The third test of the water trial occurred in the throne room of the palace. Although the Great Oz did not like to give audiences, he was interested in Dorothy. She wore the Silver Shoes, the talisman of the wicked Witch of the East, and bore a mark on her forehead, the sign of the protection of the good Witch of the North, suggesting that her power was not a threat to the good, but a boon. When Dorothy entered the throne room, she saw a gigantic head and heard the dread command of Oz that she kill the Wicked Witch of the West. When the Scarecrow went for his interview with the Great Oz, he saw instead a beautiful winged lady, but the command was the same. The Tin Woodman and the Cowardly Lion experienced even stranger apparitions in their interviews: a beast with ten limbs and a ball of fire. The combined experiences of Dorothy and her three companions corresponded roughly with what the farmer had told them to expect. Their host had said that the Great Oz appeared to his countrymen as a bird, an elephant, a cat, and a beautiful fairy.

Oz informed each supplicant that meeting their requests required that they first perform a certain service. The true test of feeling occurred in the throne room as the Wizard assigned a mission to each companion that seemed impossible to accomplish. Dorothy and her companions a now faced a dilemma: Should they obey the command of the Wizard or give up their quests? When they had taken up their first mission, they had simply followed the advice of the good Witch of the North and stayed on the road of yellow brick. In the land of the Munchkins, the three companions were each tested individually and then together when, at the chasm, they joined their abilities to complete the first stage of the path, the fire trial of thinking, or common sense. In the Land of Oz they accomplished the test of crossing the river and the test of the poppy field before entering the throne room for the third and final test of the second stage of self-development, the water trial of feeling. The prospect of yet a third stage of their journey left them confused and afraid. This future trial offered no clear path to follow, and the necessity of doing a deed that was both terribly dangerous and abhorrent—killing the Wicked Witch.

The spirit pupil might well abandon the path of self-development at this juncture. Setting forth onto the third stage of initiation requires becoming open to a kind of inner guidance. No external restraint compels the pupil at this turn; the motive force comes from within. Nor is it required that the spirit pupil take up this third trial, which involves a series of tests of willing or volition. The quest may be abandoned at this point, though Dorothy and her companions opted to go forward at the instigation of the Lion, whose fame as a coward was perhaps diminished thereby.

# Chapter 5

# THE THREE COMPANIONS
## AND THE ANTEBELLUM SOCIAL CLASSES

A review of Dorothy's three companions may prove beneficial before delving further into her journey. In particular, a fairy tale by Germany's greatest writer helps to shed light on Baum's own tale, written a hundred years later. Goethe called his fairy tale "The Green Snake and the Beautiful Lily." The Beautiful Lily was much like Dorothy, and her three companions were called the three handmaidens. Goethe's tale had four kings whose temple would rise up when the time was right, and who were bound up with the four cardinal directions in a fashion similar to the four witches in Baum's tale. Whereas in Baum's tale a great desert separates the earthly realm of Kansas from the soul world of Oz, in "The Green Snake" a great river divides the earthly realm from Lily's realm. Goethe begins his tale in a way similar to that of Baum and introduces his reader to an old woman and her dog, Mops, and an old man with a lamp, as if Toto had somehow stayed behind when Dorothy was carried off to the Land of Oz. Such similarities are more than casual. Connecting Goethe's Green Snake to the Great Oz illuminates the relationships of twelve characters in each fairy tale to one another.

## The Three Companions

In 1910, ten years after Baum wrote his modern fairy tale, Rudolf Steiner wrote "The Portal of Initiation," a play that was consciously indebted to Goethe's tale. His subtitle was "A Rosicrucian Mystery through Rudolf Steiner." In the introduction he actually included a list of the characters in his play and drew comparisons to their counterparts in Goethe's tale. When a chart of characters from Goethe and Steiner's works includes those of Baum's in a third column, strong parallels emerge. They suggest that the inspiring spirit that Baum felt had helped him might well be the same one that Steiner felt had inspired both himself and Goethe.

| THE WIZARD OF OZ | THE GREEN SNAKE AND THE BEAUTIFUL LILY | THE PORTAL OF INITIATION |
|---|---|---|
| | *Four Companions* | |
| Dorothy with Scarecrow Cowardly Lion Tin Woodman | Beautiful Lily with The Three Handmaidens | Maria with Luna Astrid Philia |
| *Four Witches* | *Four Kings* | *Four Initiates* |
| Witch of the North Witch of the East Glinda the Good Wicked Witch | Gold King Silver King Copper King Mixed King | Benedictus Theodosius Romanus Retardus |
| *Kansas & Omaha* | *Earthly Realm* | *Atavistically Gifted* |
| Aunt Em Uncle Henry The Great Oz Toto | Old Woman Old Man Green Snake Mops / Hawk | Felicia Balde Felix Balde Other Maria Theodora |

The idea that the incidents of Dorothy's journey through the Land of Oz represent historical occurrences in America appeared first, as the Introduction discussed, in an essay by Henry Littlefield. His identification of the Tin Woodman with the industrial workers relates the axe-wielding machine-man to the force of willing or volition. He helps to clarify the Cowardly Lion as the soul force of feeling by equating him with Populism at the turn of the twentieth century and the emerging middle class. Littlefield's discussion of the Scarecrow and the farmers completes his picture of society and its division into industry, politics, and agriculture.

A tremendous expansion of manufacturing came about in America as one result of the Civil War. The years after the war saw an extraordinary growth in all areas of industry, including railroad building, oil exploration, and shipbuilding. The general business conditions, however, were untamed and chaotic. The railroads spread with much waste of material, manpower and capital, a testimony to the arrogance and avarice of their builders. Fares, freight prices, and schedules fluctuated wildly and sometimes illogically. Railroad owners and their business partners duplicated train routes in order to undercut their competitors and force them out of business. The Railroad Acts of 1862 and 1864, which granted land on alternate sides of the train tracks, were promoted and abused by most railroad entrepreneurs. The so-called robber barons—men like Gould, Vanderbilt, Harriman, and Rockefeller—enriched themselves in the process.

The rampant individualism in all branches of the economy had the effect of cutting off each limb from the economic whole. The strange fate of the Tin Woodman presents a picture of this process. As the wicked Witch of the East turned his own axe against him and severed his limbs, a tinsmith replaced each lost limb with one made of tin. The result was the Tin Woodman, who, now made completely of tin, feared that he had lost his heart. Whereas the laborer had once affirmed his humanity by being productive and creative in his work, now his job threatened to turn him into a machine, and the result of his craft became an alien product. The railroad gangs living in shanty towns were only one aspect of the mechanization of labor in all areas of industry. The ever-present danger of layoffs compounded the threat of this dehumanizing labor. The Tin Woodman had to keep his oil-can with him at all times because of this danger of paralysis. The industrialization of America was accompanied by periodic depressions, financial panics, and cutthroat competition that turned unemployed workers into paralyzed machines.

The passage of the Homestead Act and the Railroad Acts showed how the Lincoln administration hoped to realize the ideal of Reconstruction in the West. Free land and easy transportation to markets were meant to assist the farmer and encourage agriculture. Those farmers who faced difficulties or who wished to expand their successful enterprises were meant to receive loans from the landbanks, whose available money could be increased by the government simply authorizing more greenbacks to be printed. In Baum's picture of the Scarecrow, the sad outcome of these policies becomes apparent. In the East, Reconstruction failed those workers who put in sixty-hour weeks only to owe their souls to the company store. So too did it fail in the West. Farmers contended with the corruption of landbanks and the chaos of railroad construction, as well as the weather. The Scarecrow, like the Tin Woodman, is one of Baum's "meatless" characters. He is the creation not of the tin-smith, but of the farmer himself. If the Tin Woodman shows the mechanization of labor, then the Scarecrow reveals the "new man" who once had acted out of new principles (as the French historian, Crevecoeur, observed of Americans at the time of the Revolutionary War), but now resembled a helpless, hapless figure stuck on a pole in the middle of a cornfield.

The plight of the farmer is akin to that of the industrial worker in that both are immobilized. Baum describes how the Scarecrow is tormented by crows that no longer fear him. In the South, the plight of the farmer was exactly that. Former slaves who once had hoped for forty acres and a mule became sharecroppers hemmed in by the racist Jim Crow laws. The laws of segregation even took away their vote, making the Southern farmer truly powerless.

The supporters of greenbacks were often aligned with those people who wished to coin silver in a fixed equivalency rate to gold. Adopting a silver standard would help to free the American monetary system from the European bankers' control. However, neither greenbacks nor silver coins were allowed back into circulation in any abundance. European bankers preferred to have currency backed by gold, which they controlled. Their influence resulted eventually in the "Crime of '73," as the demonetization of silver was later named, which ironically was signed into law by President Grant on Lincoln's birthday. An economic depression followed immediately. These downturns and panics repeated themselves periodically.

A further consequence of the monetary policies that abolished greenbacks and reverted to the gold standard involved the debts incurred by the government. European bankers were only too happy to service these debts at an interest rate of six per cent. President Garfield moved to take away the Morgan bank's monopoly to sell U.S. bonds. He wanted to put them on the open market and lower the interest rate to four per cent. His assassination on July 2, 1881, ended his attempt to regain control of monetary policy. European bankers loaned huge sums of money for the industrialization of America and especially railroad construction. Bankers dealing with Junior Morgan in London and J.P. Morgan in New York financed railroad bonds and demanded repayment in gold. The gold reserves of the U.S. government were frequently in danger of getting too low. This situation reached a climax in 1895 when the U.S. Treasury was three weeks away from running out. President Cleveland had to borrow gold from J.P. Morgan and Augustus Belmont to bail out the government.

The American Bimetallic League and the Populist Party stirred up public sentiment with political meetings in St. Louis and Chicago. William Jennings Bryan, a congressman from Nebraska, emerged as a fervent proponent of silver. Bryan proved himself to be a powerful orator and became the Democratic Presidential candidate opposed to McKinley. Littlefield's interpretation of *The Wizard of Oz* identified the Cowardly Lion with Bryan himself. The Lion is indeed a "meat character," and the idea that the voice of the people might speak through him has a certain merit to it. The secret of the character of the Lion is that he too had changed, though not into straw or tin. The Lion shows a picture of a middle class emerging in the towns and cities of America that has become filled with fear. Whereas the rightful domain of activity for the Tin Woodman is the factory, and for the Scarecrow the farmer's field, the domain of the Lion is the town—the social realm—and the political arena in particular. The Lion of the populace roared often in marches of protest and in torchlight parades such as those L. Frank Baum joined in 1896. But a feeling of paralysis was as much a part of these gatherings as the immobility suffered by the Scarecrow in his field or the Tin Woodman rusted by the rain. A disenchantment with the political system was pervasive. Grant's Crime of '73 pales before the scope of corruption in his cabinet or that of the Tweed Ring in New York City. The situation a century later, when not even one-half of eligible voters participated in the national election, was actually an improvement.

The following chart attempts to summarize the history of Reconstruction in relation to how Baum portrays each of Dorothy's three companions.

| **Character**<br>(*Soul Element*) | **Manifestation**<br>**in Society** | **Social**<br>**Class** | **Ideal of**<br>**Lincoln** |
|---|---|---|---|
| Scarecrow<br>(*Reason*) | Western Farmer<br>*Southern*<br>*Sharecropper* | Farmer | Homestead Act<br>Railroad Act<br>Landbanks |
| Cowardly Lion<br>(*Enspirited*) | Urban Small<br>Businessman | Middle<br>Class | Freedman's Bureau<br>Greenbacks |
| Tin Woodman<br>(*Volition*) | Coal Miners<br>Railroad Workers<br>Factory Workers | Working<br>Class | Reconstruction |

chapter 6

# THE WICKED WITCH OF THE WEST

---

When Dorothy and her three companions arrived in the Country of the Winkies, they discovered that it was rough, hilly, and untilled. The Country of the Munchkins had appeared quite civilized with its road of yellow brick, well-kept homes, and carefully tended farmlands, but here the land was empty and wild. The contrast of the Country of the Winkies with the Emerald City was even starker, for in the latter the people lived in a well-organized society, a teeming city with a proper leader. The Wicked Witch stood behind the untamed aspect of the soul world of the Winkies. Her rulership over the Western Land had prevented the Winkies from inhabiting it in a healthful way. Her reign may also be connected with the strange qualities of the gray landscape of Kansas, where the evil witch's fear of water and of the dark seemed to have seeped down into the very soil. The arid dimness was so pervasive that no relief seemed possible. Thought itself led to despair for the "hollow men," the scarecrow men.

T.S. Eliot's masterpiece characterizes these qualities of the Wicked Witch quite clearly. In "The Waste Land," in the second stanza of the fifth part, he paints the spiritual background of the American continent:

> Here is no water but only rock
> Rock and no water and the sandy road
> The road winding above among the mountains
> Which are mountains of rock without water
> If there were water we should stop and drink
> Amongst the rocks one cannot stop or think
> Sweat is dry and feet are in the sand
> If there were only water amongst the rock
> Dead mountain mouth of carious teeth that
>     cannot spit
> Here one can neither stand nor lie nor sit
> There is not even silence in the mountains
> But dry sterile thunder without rain
> There is not even solitude in the mountains
> But red sullen faces sneer and snarl
> From doors of mudcracked houses

The decision to take up the third trial of initiation, commonly referred to as the air trial, necessarily leads to taking action. The pupil must attain decisiveness. Finding just the right action for a given situation requires the development of this virtue. What Dorothy and her companions will face in the Country of the Winkies amount to surprise attacks, not events they could prepare for. These attacks resemble the death of the wicked Witch of the East in that earthly events (like the end of serfdom in Russia) can be understood more deeply when related to them. The air trial reflects the activity of the soul forces and the ego attaining decisiveness, and mirrors the social classes and folk soul working downward from spirit heights to infuse the social organism with this virtue.

The events on the road of yellow brick that occurred before the meeting with the Great Oz can properly be viewed as a description of the spiritual background of American history from the Civil War up to the beginning of the twentieth century. The Populist view, however, needs to be interpreted more narrowly as a characterization of the effects of capitalist expansion on farmers, industrial workers, and the middle class. Dorothy's journey reveals how the Witch's inspirations stand behind the disenfranchisement of the Southern sharecropper, the oppression of the labor movement, and the corruption of the political process. Twisting Baum's tale of meeting the three companions and coming to the Emerald City into a political allegory can hide the important element of prophecy in this tale. The incidents that bring Dorothy and her companions into conflict with the Wicked Witch and her minions belong to the history of the twentieth and twenty-first centuries. They constitute the prophetic element of *The Wonderful Wizard of Oz*.

The history of American slavery provides insight into the character of the Wicked Witch of the West: her desire to enslave and her hatred of freedom. The slave trade was based on racism, the false idea that the Caucasian race is inherently superior to the Negroid one. The dissemination of this lie enabled Great Britain to establish the Golden Triangle of the Atlantic trade routes. The lie itself was a distortion of the occult truth about the origin of the races found in the Akasha Chronicle, the spiritual record of historical events or what religion calls the Book of Life. Certain Western secret societies that rose to power in England at the beginning of the seventeenth century intentionally misused and distorted this knowledge. These groups, and the monarchs that served their goals, were a kind of repetition of events in Roman times and worked in the background to shape the emergence of the British Empire. Just as Roman emperors like Nero and Caligula demanded that the mystery centers of Rome grant them initiation and then misused the powers such rites conferred, so did the English kings employ racism to justify the atrocities of the slave trade. The mythological She-wolf stands as a picture of the spiritual impulse that reigned over Roman history and led to the evil excesses epitomized by the gladiatorial contests. Dante's *Divine Comedy*, the defining epic of medieval Italy, begins with the threat that the She-wolf poses to Dante's journey and the warning by Dante's guide, Virgil, to forego opposing her power. The She-wolf also appears in *Beowulf*, the medieval Anglo-Saxon epic. She is the mother of Grendel, the Water Witch whom Beowulf, the great hero of his people, has to vanquish. The progress of this evil impulse from Rome to Northern Europe, thence to England, and finally to America, may help to clarify the nature of the Idea at work in the machinations of the Western secret societies.

The telescopic eye of the Wicked Witch provides the means by which she gains knowledge of any attempt to oppose her power. Government spying in America reflects this strange power of the Wicked Witch. When the Federal Bureau of Investigation was founded in the 1920s, J. Edgar Hoover began assembling intelligence files on tens of thousands of American citizens. In the 1960s he used these files to determine which leaders to neutralize as part of COINTELPRO, the FBI's far-reaching plan to disrupt civil rights organizations with operations to assassinate Black leaders such as Fred Hampton. The expansion of governmental eavesdropping by the NSA under President Bush dwarfed all previous efforts in this direction. In his novel, *1984*, George Orwell gave the classic presentation of the power of the Wicked Witch in the figure of Big Brother, who used spying to deprive citizens of all human freedom. The Witch's spyglass enabled her to identify Dorothy and recognize the great threat that she posed—that she was as dangerous as the Great Oz himself, and that she had to be destroyed. In addition to her telescopic eye, the evil witch possessed a second talisman of power. Her silver whistle was the counterpart of the Silver Shoes that had once belonged to the wicked Witch of the East. While the Silver Shoes could send away any threat to the eastern Witch and banish it to another realm, the whistle could call servants who would protect its owner and do her dirty work.

Baum's pictures of the five attacks of the Wicked Witch against Dorothy and her companions form the prophecy of the twentieth and twenty-first centuries that is embedded in Baum's tale. Baum's picture-language presents the evil nature of the minions that serve their queen, the erstwhile She-wolf. Rudolf Steiner undertook research into the plans of the Western secret societies—namely, those occult groups that would use their knowledge of spiritual beings and spiritual faculties for selfish reasons and for the benefit of a small group of people rather than for all of mankind. Some of this research was published under the title of *The Karma of Untruthfulness*, a series of twenty-five lectures given from Dec. 4, 1916 to Jan. 30, 1917. Steiner presented a broad array of facts and detailed explanations so that his listener could judge for himself or herself the truth of these plans. While it is beyond the scope of this book to take up Steiner's lectures in detail, his research will be used to help clarify the correspondences between earthly events and their spiritual counterparts in *The Wonderful Wizard of Oz*.

Steiner gave these lectures with the hope that knowledge of the plans of the Western secret societies would allow human beings to become free from the untruthfulness that they are based upon. In simplest terms, such secret societies, like the Wicked Witch herself, want to enslave people. Steiner, by contrast, saw himself as a fighter for freedom. He disagreed with these plans, but felt that they must be understood in order to make sense of the dire and earth-shattering events that would follow World War I, "the war to end all wars." The fundamental belief held by these groups is that the English-speaking peoples are destined to become the leaders of the new age. The term they use to characterize the dominant people of each age is "sub-race." They refer to the previous age as the Roman sub-race. They believe that in its first stage the Roman sub-race formed the Roman Empire through military power and ruled over the Germanic tribes, who were still in their infancy. The Romans played the role of wet nurse, as it were. With the decline and fall of the Roman Empire and the ascension of the Roman Catholic Church, they maintain that the Roman sub-race attained not a military dominance, but a religious and cultural hegemony over all of Europe. The role of the Catholic Church toward the Germanic tribes became that of guardian.

Steiner indicated that the activity of the Western secret societies appeared on the stage of world history with the death of Queen Elizabeth I and the coronation in 1603 of King James I, who began teaching British superiority to his people. In his Masonic lodge, King James explained that the Roman descendants or Romance-language speaking peoples must become stragglers in this new age, which he named the Anglo-Saxon sub-race. The first stage, military dominance, would culminate in the formation of the British Empire, a global power that would be the counterpart of the Roman Empire. The second stage, cultural ascendancy, would require materialistic and technological inventions deriving from what he called occult mechanics and would depend on harnessing the native genius of the Anglo-American peoples. The transition from the first to the second stage would be difficult, since a full repetition of the Roman sub-race would require shaping the modern counterpart of the Germanic tribes—which King James thought to be the Slavic peoples—for their future role.

The British government, the hierarchy of the Anglican Church, and the British ship-builders and bankers moved to implement the King's plan. The need to build up and expand the British navy and merchant ships was paramount, since claiming far-distant colonies and controlling them was integral to transforming an island nation into an empire. The business class entered into the slave trade as a means of gaining the necessary capital to finance these various ventures. By the middle of the seventeenth century, Parliament cooperated with the King's grand design by passing the Navigation Acts, which claimed complete control of the Atlantic trade routes and restricted British colonies to trading only with Great Britain and its territories within the empire. By the beginning of the 1700s, Britain attained dominance over the Atlantic trade routes and formed what was called the "Golden Triangle." British ships carried goods from the textile factories in England to the East coast of Africa. There, merchants sold their goods at a considerable profit, with which they purchased slaves to load onto their empty ships. The Middle Passage extended across the Atlantic Ocean to the Americas, where the slaves were sold at a huge profit to plantations in both North and South America. The third leg of the triangular trade route bought raw materials, including sugar, tobacco, and cotton, back to England. The irony of the name given to this plan to make the English people the spearhead of the Industrial Revolution and the founders of an empire is that the Freemasonic lodges used this same term, the Golden Triangle, to describe the high ideal and goal of their path of thirty-three degrees—the balancing of the soul forces of thinking, feeling and willing to become the triangle of equal sides with angles that are all the same.

The tale of the Golden Triangle, as told by history, is the incredible adventure of a small island nation that achieved a great victory to become the central hub of a vast empire that stretched around the globe, a veritable recreation of the Roman

Empire. This empire, grand though it became, was founded on a lie. The misnomer, as it were, began with secret teachings that identified the present age as "the Anglo-Saxon sub-race." The present age, in truth, has the task of creating a culture that can help men and women to attain freedom, not to form a master race. Creating such a culture requires an educational system that brings the greatness of all cultures into the purview of its students. The fact that prejudice against other cultures exists today shows that the education of the human race still has far to go. More pernicious than this lie of the sub-race, however, is the deep-seated racism it engenders, for such dark bias aligns with the purposes of the Wicked Witch to enslave people. The self-evident truth that exists in the words, "All men are created equal," can be difficult to recognize. Our present age is dedicated to this high ideal through the spirit of the Founding Fathers and their devotion to the Spirit of Liberty, Columbia. Thomas Jefferson and John Adams even died on the same day, July fourth, 1826, fifty years to the day after they ushered her onto the stage of world history with the Declaration of Independence.

The prevalence of the lie that one race is better or greater than another obscures a proper understanding of modern plantation slavery. The Anglican religion was complicit in spreading this lie, though Catholicism did little to oppose it. To enlist the God of Love in defense of slavery is futile. The full meaning of the sacrifice of the god who became man will gradually unfold to humanity, but the philosopher Hegel, the most famous of the German Idealists, insisted that only the spirit of those human beings who are fully awake and self-conscious could be witness to its truth. Hegel characterized the initial experience of this Idea, for those persons who are awake to its import, as the dawning of the spirit of brotherhood. Love for one's fellow man flows out of the sacrifice of the God of Love. This love foreshadows the end of slavery, for the principle of freedom in human relationships sustains the freely given offer of grace for all human beings.

Modern plantation slavery as it manifested in the sixteenth through nineteenth centuries should be viewed as an aberration, an attempt to revive an institution that died out in Europe in the 1200s. The modern English word "slavery" comes from the Middle English word "sclave," or "Slav," used to refer to people living in Eastern Europe in the latter half of the Greco-Roman age (a more appropriate term that recognizes the contributions of the ancient Greeks to Western culture). Slaves were Slavs who were defeated in battle and forced to serve their conquerors. In Western Europe, the feudal class of serfs emerged at the end of the Greco-Roman cultural age to replace slaves. By contrast, modern plantation slavery came about purely for the sake of self-interested profit and greed.

The leaders of the Western secret societies had a different view of what the Slavic peoples needed. They believed that the Slavs were the modern counterpart to the Germanic tribes during the Roman sub-race, those tribes that first had the Roman Empire as a wet nurse and then the Roman Catholic Church as a guardian. During the reign of King Henry VIII of

England, the Church withdrew. With the ascension of King James I, the kingdom of Great Britain entered upon its adulthood. In the seventeenth century, Great Britain took steps to increase its activity in the slave trade and in investment in colonization. By the next century, the British would take over trade routes and formally begin the Industrial Revolution. With the defeat of Napoleon at Waterloo in 1814, Wellington removed the final impediment to completing the first stage of King James's plan. During the reign of Queen Victoria, the British expanded into Asia—first into China by fighting the Opium War and forcing the Chinese to include the drug in their economy, and secondly into India by playing native factions against each other and using modern weapons of war to subdue them when necessary. Soon the sun never set on British soil.

The goal of forming an empire was not the plan's culmination, but only the end of a stage. Such an insight helps to clarify the transition to the second stage of the plan, the broad outlines and purposes of which need to become intelligible. Just as religious faith gave unity to Europe and granted a certain hegemony to the Roman Catholic Church in the Middle Ages, so did the Western secret societies envision that the hidden talents of the English-speaking peoples for ingenuity and innovation could be twisted to form a materialistic, highly technological culture where movies and TV are replacing literature and books; where typing and tapping are replacing writing and literacy; where electronic music and recordings are replacing listening to orchestras; and where sports are becoming king. The threat to the cultural hegemony that the servants of the Wicked Witch desired came mainly from Germany. German culture, and Idealism in particular, offered a viable alternative to mass media and the manufactured reality of commercial entertainment and had to be opposed. A plan to attack German culture, especially with the new impetus that infused it at the beginning of the twentieth century, had to accompany the plan for the Slavic peoples. The Western secret societies employed a kind of sleight-of-hand so that the "socialist experiment," as it was called, should not appear connected to them in any way. Maps that began to appear in the 1890s showed the various republics of Europe, but diminished the East with the label of the "Russian Desert," laying the groundwork for the October Revolution and the overthrow of the czar more than a quarter of a century later.

*Detail from "The Kaiser's Dream", The Truth, London, 1890. Maps imitating this original appeared in publications from England to Germany.*

## Chapter 7

# THE GOLDEN CAP,
## Modern Plantation Slavery,
## and the Mexican War

Before Dorothy and her companions left the City of Oz, the Guardian of the Gate told her that she need not worry about how to find the Wicked Witch, "for when she knows you are in the Country of the Winkies she will find you, and make you all her slaves." The heartless cruelty of the Witch of the West and her rulership over the Winkies may be compared with the dominion of the Witch of the East over the Munchkins. Both witches enslaved their peoples, although the enslavement of the Winkies was apparently worse since it robbed them of anything like the warm family life of the Munchkins. If the bondage of the Munchkins relates to the presence of serfdom in Russia, then that of the Winkies reflects the institution of slavery in America. Baum reveals that the Witch of the West brought about the horrible enslavement of the Winkies through her first use of the Golden Cap, a magical device with a charm set on it that allowed the wearer to call upon a crowd of Winged Monkeys who were required to follow any command given to them. The Wicked Witch unleashed the Winged Monkeys to create a form of slavery more twisted than the binding of the serfs to the land of Mother Russia. The slave trade that produced

American slavery began in 1619 in Jamestown, a year before the arrival of the Pilgrims on Plymouth Rock in a town named after the British king. Slave narratives by the victims of England's plan give testimony of the horrors of the Middle Passage, the ocean voyage on the slave ships. Having landed in America, the shipmasters took their human cargo to slave markets, where families were broken apart as mothers, fathers, and children were sold off to different plantations.

In the Country of the Winkies, Dorothy discovered the great cruelty and fear that the Wicked Witch used to terrorize and rule over the people. The Witch embodied the darkest threat faced by the people of the West, in a very real way the anti-spirit to Dorothy's benevolence. The cause of the great Civil War in America—the cyclone that swept Dorothy away—was slavery. In his draft of the Declaration of Independence, Thomas Jefferson had characterized the evil of slavery as the worst of all the injustices that required the American colonists to revolt against King George III. Although this version of the Declaration was not sent to the king, Jefferson required that its contents be preserved:

> [The King] has waged cruel war against human nature itself, violating its most sacred rights of life and liberty in the persons of a distant people who never offended him, captivating and carrying them into slavery in another hemisphere, or to incur miserable death in their transportation thither. This piratical warfare, the opprobrium of INFIDEL Powers, is the warfare of the CHRISTIAN king of Great Britain. Determined to keep open a market

where MEN should be bought and sold, he has prostituted his negative for suppressing every legislative attempt to prohibit or to restrain this execrable commerce. And that this assemblage of horrors might want no fact of distinguished die, he is now exciting those very people to rise in arms among us, and to purchase that liberty of which he has deprived them, by murdering the people on whom he also obtruded them: thus paying off former crimes committed against the LIBERTIES of one people, with crimes which he urges them to commit against the LIVES of another.[4]

Baum's description of the crowd of monkeys that appears at the Witch's side, "each with a pair of immense and powerful wings on his shoulders," indicates that these strange creatures belong to a different stage of evolution than the earthly one that humankind is currently passing through. They are below the stage of man (they are monkeys), but above that of animals (they have wings). Their intent is to create humor, a kind of persistent practical joke that goes over like a lead balloon, but the result is demonic. In chapter 14 of Baum's book, the king of the Winged Monkeys explains to Dorothy how the forces of good brought them under the sway of the Golden Cap, and how the Wicked Witch later gained control of the Cap and used its power to order the Winged Monkeys to help her enslave the Land of the Winkies. The story that history tells of the Middle Passage is difficult to hold credible: an estimate of a twenty per cent death rate on board the slave ships would mean that the transport of 400,000 slaves to the

American colonies by 1750 resulted in 100,000 murders. The slave traders either believed the black race to be sub-human, or they lacked a conscience, or both. The possibility that Baum's tale asks us to entertain is that the release of the Winged Monkeys in the seventeenth century resulted in the possession of these slave traders. Their madness and cruelty, documented in slave narratives, would thereby find an explanation.

An article in the 1970 edition of the *Encyclopedia Britannica* on "Slavery" attempted to clarify how modern plantation slavery is different from the slavery that died out in Europe in the Middle Ages, and from the vestiges of slavery that can be found on other continents in modern times. It holds the Anglican Church responsible for establishing the color line— one of the worst aspects of plantation slavery. The existence of the color line signifies that a deep-seated racism had corrupted the very laws of the land, somehow managing to twist the meaning of "law-abiding citizen" into "defender of evil." By transporting two million slaves from 1680 to 1780, the British were responsible for half a million murders and condemning millions more to the racism, torture, and rape that seemed to so delight slave breakers and slave masters.

The political upheaval that broke the British Empire's political control over its former colonies did not seem to affect the system of slavery that had taken root there. How England got the colonies to accept the slave trade in the first place helps to explain why slavery continued in America after the Revolutionary War. In order for the Golden Triangle to be successful, the slave dealers in Africa, the crews manning the slave ships, and the slave masters in America all had to subscribe to the belief that their work involved creatures who were less-than-human. The personal narratives of Africans who were swept up into the slave trade continually stress their abhorrence, not of slavery itself, but of the inhuman form of American plantation slavery. Africans who had lived as slaves in native tribes always felt that they were human beings, but the racism they experienced in the Middle Passage made them feel like monstrous devils had seized hold of their masters. It was not the necessarily the institution of slavery itself that confounded the Founding Fathers, but the scourge of racism that had infected the minds of too many of their fellow citizens.

The power of this racist ideology was not broken by the defeat of the Slave Power in the Civil War, but neither could the source of the South's power remain hidden. With the appearance of the Ku Klux Klan after the Civil War, a reign of terror spread over the South. The Jim Crow laws became the legal expression of the rule of the Ku Klux Klan over the politics of the South both during and after Reconstruction. Lincoln's ideal for peaceful reunification did not prevail. The Hayes Compromise ended Reconstruction, and the policy of segregation became the *post bellum* visage of the racism that had justified the slave trade and allowed the institution of slavery to be incorporated in the Constitution. The secret rites and ceremonies of the Klan helped to inculcate a mindless mob mentality in its adherents. Lynching, tar-and-feathering, and cross-burning drove home the distorted belief in the supremacy of the white race that Klansmen were expected to adopt.

The power of this racist ideology must be viewed spiritually. Its ability to withstand the defeat of the South in the Civil War showed that it was not bound to any single institution, policy, or organization. Rather, it was bound to the Wicked Witch herself. It was a minion that served her. The twisted thinking that this racism entailed suggests that it was a creation of the Witch that, through certain occult practices, was made to possess the souls of human beings. The Crows are a picture of human thinking distorted by her evil. The first use of the Golden Cap enabled the Wicked Witch to force the Winkies into slavery. Her command over the Crows enabled her to perpetuate it. When the legal and formal basis of slavery was finally overthrown, it was no wonder that a secret society emerged in the South to spread its racist underpinnings by twisting the minds of its members with the idea of white supremacy. The evil force of soul that possessed these individuals even manifested in the very name of the laws they passed to enforce their distorted point of view—Jim Crow.

Baum tells us that the Wicked Witch unleashed the Winged Monkeys a second time. The primary purpose of this second use of the cap was to drive out Oz, who at that time lived in Omaha, not far from the plains of Kansas. Her use of the Golden Cap before the advent of the Civil War had the effect of strengthening what Lincoln knew as the Slave Power Conspiracy. The South had become something other than what the Founding Fathers had hoped. The U.S. Constitution granted slave owners an additional three-fifths of a vote for each slave. Getting elected in the South became increasingly a question of how many slaves one owned. By the time of the Missouri Compromise in 1820, political power had gradually fallen into the hands of slave owners. Politics, and the social sphere in general, came under the sway of the economic necessity of owning slaves. The leaders of the Democratic Party tightened their grip on the source of their power. A form of religious fundamentalism, which had once flourished in the North as Puritanism, emerged in the South as a counter-image of Transcendentalism. Religious leaders completed the task of joining the cotton economy and slave-based politics with a racist culture. It was Southern politicians, however, who decided to expand slavery at all costs.

*The Slave Power Conspiracy* is the name of an influential book that appeared just before the Civil War. It tells the truth about the Alamo in 1836 and the war with Mexico that soon followed, pointing out the fact that Texas wished to become a slave state, while Mexico wanted to eliminate slavery. The plan of the Slave Power was to provoke the Mexican army and go to war to gain more land from Mexico so that slavery could extend to the Pacific Ocean. In order to reach this goal, a war with Mexico had to be somehow manufactured. Selling the jingoism of "Remember the Alamo" proved to be very successful. The *Memoirs* of Ulysses S. Grant, who participated in the war as an officer in the invading force, tells the truth about the fabricated war and how American troops reigned terror down on Mexican soldiers. The United States Congress, having just gained Democratic majorities in both houses and a Democratic President in the White House, declared war on Mexico in

1845, the same year that Transcendentalism faded away. At the war's end, when the treaty of 1848 was signed, over one-half of the land mass of Old Mexico was turned over to the possession of the United States. The pro-slavery party had a clear idea of how such new land could be put to best use by spreading slavery to the West. Baum offers up a picture of the Wizard floating away from Omaha in a balloon, the counterpart of Dorothy's cyclone. Perhaps the loss of the spirit of Idealism in America hints at a deeper loss of the spirit of Neoclassicism, precipitated by the theft of one-half of Mexico's land.

Although no compromise could be wrung from Southern politicians, President Lincoln could not accept the idea of allowing the South to go its own way. By holding to the goal of saving the Union, he brought an end to its gravest evil. In the process he defeated many of America's best generals and her most heroic soldiers. His vision for Reconstruction should be judged in the light of what he himself proposed, not how other Presidents, bowing to quite other goals, actually brought about the opposite. More importantly, Lincoln attempted to deny the forces of capitalism control of the political sphere. The Civil War produced a debt of three billion dollars, but Lincoln's genius arrived at a solution—the greenback. The government itself would take on this debt, rather than let it fall into the hands of private financiers. This idea is the seed that Lincoln bequeathed the future. It also lies at the heart of Littlefield's Populist interpretation of *The Wonderful Wizard of Oz*.

# Chapter 8

# THE ATTACK OF THE WOLVES
## and Bolshevism

When the Wicked Witch of the West looked out with her one eye that was as powerful as a telescope and saw that Dorothy had come into her land and was resting for the night, she became angry. She blew once upon her silver whistle, and a pack of great Wolves appeared to do her bidding. She ordered them to kill Dorothy and her companions. The Wolves are a symbol of man's animal nature and the fierceness of the human will, or what Plato called the appetitive nature of man. The Tin Woodman was awake to their threat and used his axe to defend Dorothy while she slept. After forty blows of his axe, forty Wolves lay dead, and the Tin Woodman had defeated this threat.

The Witch's first attack reflects the "socialist experiment" that the Western secret societies had been planning since the 1880s, which began the transition from the British Empire to the second stage of their plan. The October Revolution took place only months after Steiner's lecture cycle, *The Karma of Untruthfulness*, which clearly warned of the dire consequences of what would come to be known as Bolshevism. The establishment of a Bolshevik Russia, the Union of Soviet Socialist Republics, also occurred as a direct result of American intervention in World War I. Vladimir Lenin was allowed to travel through Germany with the understanding that a Leninist Russia would sign a peace treaty with Germany, allowing it to combine all its forces and face the American Expeditionary Force that was coming to France. General Ludendorff, Germany's military dictator, made the fateful decision to send Lenin and his cell of Marxists through Germany in a railway car on their way from Switzerland to Russia in April of 1917. Ludendorff had military reasons to justify his action, especially Lenin's promise of neutrality and Germany's need to fight a single-front war against the nations of Western Europe. The socialist experiment became a world historic event with the October Revolution of 1917. American ships stationed in the Baltic Sea did not intervene on the side of the White Russians as Lenin's small band of Communists seized power. The nightmare of Bolshevism descended upon Russia.

Bringing communism onto the stage of world history required a conceptual framework as well as a social movement. Karl Marx had actively shouldered this task in the nineteenth century, but his attempt to turn Hegel on his head was a philosophical failure. Only the sorry state of economic theory at the time made his book, *Das Kapital*, seem to be a fairly good effort. Marx's effort to characterize the capitalist economy and to portray its antithesis in the political sphere as the rise of socialism, without trying to find their synthesis, served to renounce philosophy, rather than advance it to the idea of a three-fold society. By calling for a "dictatorship of the proletariat" as a transitional stage to achieve the goal of a classless society, Marx showed how opposed to freedom he actually was. Despite its philosophical weakness, Lenin found that Marxism suited his purposes, and he did advance it conceptually in a significant way. In *Imperialism: the Highest Stage of Capitalism*, he described what actually had happened economically in the creation of the British Empire, and his prognosis was correct—that it would collapse. Lenin did not seem to suspect the actual direction that capitalism would take by becoming a global economy.

Vladimir Lenin well understood that in a dictatorship, someone must be the dictator—namely himself. The man who would succeed Lenin in power grasped this idea even more concretely. As the general secretary of the Communist Party under Lenin, Joseph Stalin wrote what came to be called "the party line." Two years after Lenin's death in 1924, Stalin put a series of brutal policies into action, including industrializing Russia by requiring people to move into cities; relocating peasant farmers into collectives and eliminating people who would not cooperate; scorching the earth when Germany invaded Russia during the Second World War; and consolidating power by using purges to get rid of anyone who might pose a threat. Stalin was noted for his cruelty. Even on his deathbed he was planning a purge that would have executed over a million people. The conservative estimate of the number of people who died as a result of his policies approaches ten million. Over twenty-eight million more were imprisoned, deported, or exiled. Stalin's radical expansion of state-run forced labor camps even resulted in the addition of a new word to the dictionary—gulag.

The true nature of Bolshevism unfolded under Stalin's leadership. The purges of the 1930s showed the cruelty that was at the heart of the man of steel. Like the contests in the Roman Coliseum, the slaughter of millions of Russian peasants who refused collectivization revealed the Wolf, whose ravenous bloodlust could not be sated. Something like the possession of the slavers and shipmasters of the Golden Triangle seems to have happened also in Russia, particularly in the case of those charged with correcting "mistaken" political tendencies—the commissars. While the Cold War is traditionally portrayed as a great battle between capitalism and communism, the collapse of the Soviet Union in 1991 without a shot being fired demonstrated that communism did not appeal to the Russian people, and that the ideal of Bolshevism—the Socialist Man—had never taken root.

Littlefield correctly interprets the Tin Woodman as a symbol for the industrial workers of America. These workers embody the positive aspect of the human will. The battle pitting the Woodman against the Wolves may thus appear as positive and negative aspects of the same soul force opposed against one another—the companion of Dorothy against the minions of the Wicked Witch. Following the Civil War, industrial workers began to organize and formed a new social movement in America. The historical meaning of Baum's fairy tale—which Littlefield and like-minded critics hoped to illuminate—needs to be viewed in relation to the Platonic idea that the soul nature of the individual is writ large in the social organism as a whole. The will nature of man symbolized by the Tin Woodman's axe finds its external counterpart in the working class, active historically in the Union Movement. The founding of the American Federation of Labor (AFL) in 1888 signaled a shift in the labor movement from the idealism of the Knights of Labor to the pragmatism of negotiating contracts with the captains of industry and their gigantic monopolies. The threat that the prominent union leader Samuel Gompers and his successors faced was actually the danger that communism posed. The task of union organizers was to gain the right of workers to negotiate with American companies, not to try and destroy the companies that employed them. The companies themselves were often able to turn aside the efforts of unions by painting them as communistic, using the Red Scare to justify their refusal to enter into good faith negotiations. Quite the opposite of the false ideal of Marx that excused the actions of anarchists and agent provocateurs, the ideal of brotherhood that bound the organizers to the workers, and the workers to one another, was actually an American ideal, native to this land—the "band of brothers" from the chorus of "Hail, Columbia!":

> Firm, united let us be,
> Rallying round our liberty,
> As a band of brothers joined,
> Peace and safety we shall find.

Baum's tale hints that the actual battle against communism for the soul of the working class was fought in America, not in Eastern Europe. The AFL achieved victory in 1935 with the passage of the National Labor Relations Act (the NLRA). Decades of struggle to establish a workers' bill of rights culminated in this legislation. So thorough was the impact of Unionism on the social and economic life of the nation that it seemed to be a repetition of the expansion of Jeffersonian democracy, a period spanning the adoption of the U.S. Constitution in 1788 to the defeat of the National Bank in 1835. The passage of the Social Security Act and the child labor laws in the same year as the NLRA were further proof of the salutary effect of the labor movement. Providing security for workers in their old age and free education for all of the nation's youth sealed the victory of Unionism and protected workers from the danger of Bolshevism, still loose in the world. Baum's picture of the Tin Woodman slaying the Wolves while Dorothy and the Lion slept thus provides a symbol of the industrial worker in his awakened state, as he employed common sense in negotiations, persevered in the struggle, and protected the soul of America manifest in the Columbian ideal of brotherhood.

## Chapter 9

# THE ATTACK OF THE CROWS
## and Nazism

The Wicked Witch of the West was furious when she saw that her Wolves were dead, and she blew her silver whistle twice. The Witch's whistle may be compared to the one that the Queen of the mice gave to Dorothy. That whistle would bring mice—the symbol of devotion—to her aid should she need them on the path of initiation, sometimes called the path of veneration. The Witch's whistle does not call up virtues, but rather vices, the purpose of which is to block the seeker on the path. Responding to the double blast of the whistle, a flock of wild Crows, enough to darken the sky, appeared to do the Witch's bidding, and flew off at her command to kill Dorothy and her companions. This time all of the companions were awake, but the Scarecrow insisted that he should meet this second attack, and the others should lie down out of harm's way. As a companion of Dorothy, the Scarecrow represents a salutary development of thinking, one grounded in common sense, the virtue honed in the fire trial. In fairy tales, crows are a symbol of the misuse of magic for selfish purposes—black magic that accomplishes its goal by means of torture. The Scarecrow, capable now of an extraordinary advancement of thought into deed, engaged the Crows in battle.

Forty Crows flew against him, and forty times he killed a Crow by twisting its neck, until at last all were lying dead beside him.

Chapter 7 on the Golden Cap describes in detail the long activity of the Crows in the West: how they first assisted in the establishment of the slave trade through the rites and ceremonies of certain secret societies that instilled racism in their members; how their influence on the larger society grew by providing a rationale for prolonging the institution of slavery; how with the birth of the new nation they gained strength and coalesced into the Slave Power Conspiracy; and how they finally entered into public view after the defeat of the Confederacy and, as the Ku Klux Klan, took effective control of the Southern states. During its heyday in the 1920s, not only did this racist organization claim millions of members, but even unlikely places such as Colorado were known as Klan states. Writers such as the novelist Richard Wright revealed the control that the Klan exercised over the police, government, judicial system, and businesses, and how dehumanizing its instruments of torture truly were.

The Crows manifested on a global scale with the spread of Nazism in Germany. Just as the Bolshevik Revolution in 1917 signaled the appearance of the Witch's Wolves, Hitler's election as chancellor in 1933 meant that the Crows had likewise stepped forth onto the stage of world history. Once in power, Hitler and his henchmen created a cult that used some of the same methods as the KKK—torchlight parades and nighttime fire rituals—to effectively mesmerize an entire nation. Nazism soon joined forces with other fascist dictatorships and threatened to spread over Europe and Asia. The United States of course opposed Hitler's grand designs, a sign not so much of the Scarecrow's resistance than the wrath of the Witch who ruled in the West and who had no desire to be replaced by one of her minions unleashed on the other side of the globe. There is a dark irony in Bolshevik Russia—aided and abetted at its birth by Germany—rising up to oppose the army of Nazi Germany with machines of war built by Russian citizens imprisoned in Stalin's forced labor camps. America's willingness to join forces with Stalin should not seem unusual since the Wolves, even if they had been defeated at home, could still be useful abroad in reining in Nazism and then helping to divide the world into spheres of influence at Potsdam at the conclusion of World War II. The ensuing Cold War permitted the spread of American capitalism into "free" Europe and the creation of multi-national corporations, which flowed into the so-called "Third World," the undeveloped countries not affiliated with the Free World or the Communist Bloc.

The defeat of Nazism showed the entire world the evil that lay at its core—the concentration camps and the ghastly torture that took place there. The murder of six million innocent human beings could not be easily swept under the rug, even though historians have tended to avoid exploring the occult meanings of the swastika and the rites of the S.S., the special police of Nazism. Hitler himself practiced and promulgated these rites. Trevor Ravenscroft's book, *The Spear of Destiny*, made public the fundamentals of black magic that stood behind the Nazi regime. Hitler's own book, *Mein Kampf*, made a plea for Aryan supremacy—the occult, racist ideal that he espoused. The Nazi Party opened its door to Hitler in 1922. He took it over in short order and launched his bid for Germany's chancellorship in 1933. Soon thereafter, he prepared to seize control of the military and to declare himself dictator. Having carefully built up the S.S for this purpose, Hitler finally unleashed his war machine to devastating effect in 1941. By the end of the Second World War, Hitler and Stalin were jointly responsible for the deaths of over ten million civilians. Perhaps the Wicked Witch, who became further enraged at every defeat, could find some solace in the demise of her Wolves and Crows by considering the magnitude of the body counts that their infamous exemplars had achieved.

From the perspective of Baum's own time, the attacks on Dorothy by the Wolves and Crows were yet future possibilities, but we now have the ability to view them in hindsight. Through the world-historic movements of Bolshevism and Nazism, the Wolves and Crows revealed their true colors, as it were. Bolshevism and the dictatorship of the proletariat introduced Russia to communism. Stalin's misuse of the party line led to numerous violent purges of his opponents. In the 1930s the Party carried out these purges on a mass scale that imparted the Stalinist regime its peculiar terroristic character. The "five-year plans," which industrialized the Union of Soviet Socialist Republics and increased its urban population by forty-five million people, also collectivized farming. The use of forced labor camps and brutal repression against the small farmers who resisted only deepened the famines that followed, further complicating the historian's task of determining how many millions died at Stalin's hand.

In Germany, the dictator was not called General Secretary, but Führer. Both nurtured cults of the personality, but Hitler actually created an educational system based upon his vision of the myth of Aryan supremacy, the Hitler Youth. Soviet education merely eliminated freedom from its curriculum and devoted its efforts to inculcating the Socialist Man. In March of 1945, defeated on all fronts and his manic dream crumbling around him, Hitler ordered the "Final Solution" to be carried out against the German people themselves. By so reversing his early fevered pitch that native Germans were destined to claim their own "Lebensraum"—or "living space"—from foreigners and neighbors alike—he revealed the truth of National Socialism. In place of the former cultural center of Europe, Nazism bequeathed a soul-spiritless desert.

Turning our gaze back towards America, the second attack on Dorothy can be viewed as a prophecy of the second great social movement that arose in the twentieth century. After the victory of the Labor movement and the defeat of Nazism, religious leaders—especially the Baptist ministers who formed the Southern Christian Leadership Conference—inaugurated the Civil Rights Movement. Following Thurgood Marshall's achievement in Brown v. Board of Education in 1954, Dr. Martin Luther King, Jr., led his congregation and other black ministers in supporting the refusal of Rosa Parks to bow to the segregated culture that made black citizens less than human. Dr. King emphasized the importance of nonviolence in dealing with racist opponents, and advocated joining hands with white liberals to end the scourge of segregation. Not union organizers practicing common sense, but civil rights activists demonstrating tolerance—the virtue of the water trial—were the key to overthrowing the Jim Crow laws, the means by which the Crows had held sway over their victims. These activists prepared to wage peace in workshops, where participants learned first-hand the meaning of non-violent direct action. Exchanging the urge to take an eye for an eye for the conscious choice to turn the other cheek could not be taught in a day. To love thy neighbor was not an instinctive response when he unleashed attack dogs against you. Only genuine tolerance could create a force as potent as that which had manifested in the labor movement—one powerful enough to transform the heart of even a George Wallace. Only forgiveness could bind up the nation's wounds and protect the soul of America.

When the non-violent protest marches, sit-ins, and freedom rides began, some ex-servicemen picked up their weapons for self-defense, such as the Deacons for Defense. Others joined hands with a new generation of white Americans and worked to overcome the American form of Nazism with its government-sanctioned oppression by practicing an American form of resistance—non-violent civil disobedience. The high ideal that these warriors of peace served echoed forth from the precincts of the Temple of Liberty in the "I Have a Dream" oration of Dr. King in 1963, delivered on the steps of the Lincoln Memorial. Yet more work was required in order for his dream to be realized. The great battle had to move inside the Capitol Building itself, as Civil Rights activists redoubled their efforts to register voters in order to engage fully in the political arena. With the passage of the Voting Rights Act in 1965, the Civil Rights Movement achieved what Unionism had accomplished with the National Labor Relations Act of 1935.

Just as Unionism can be seen as a repetition of Jeffersonian democracy a century later, so can the Civil Rights Movement be understood as a return of the events of the Civil War in a nonviolent form after the passage of a hundred years. The period from Brown v. the Board of Education and the bus boycott in Montgomery, to Freedom summer in Mississippi and the passage of the Voting Rights Act, reflects the period from the Kansas-Nebraska Act of 1854 and John Brown's appearance in Kansas, to the passage of the thirteenth amendment and the cessation of hostilities at Appomattox in 1865. The breaking of the bars of the prison of segregation—the repeal of the Jim Crow laws—ended the grip of the wild Crows on the South and signaled the victory of the Scarecrow, a picture of religious leaders and liberals in an awakened state, exercising, in the words of Lincoln, malice towards none and charity for all, thus safe-guarding the Columbian ideal of equality and the very folk soul of America.

# Chapter 10

# THE ATTACK OF THE BLACK BEES
## and Americanism

The final three attacks of the Wicked Witch against Dorothy and her companions belong to Baum's prophecy for the twenty-first century. The Black Bees, the Winkie Army, and the Winged Monkeys are symbols of certain trends of thought that are presently active in the world, though historians find it difficult to define them precisely since history necessarily depends on a retrospective viewpoint. A proper study of such active trends of thought should keep in mind Emerson's insight that such Ideas are causes, not purposes, and are more akin to the laws of nature than the plans of human beings. Any attempt to anthropomorphize living Ideas would lead away from their deeper meaning. The task of the so-called "think tanks" that attempt to guide politics and economics in modern times is to understand future trends through a kind of symptomatology of history. Such think tanks believe that if historical events are studied as a series of symptoms that point to a knowable present condition of civilization, then one can discern the common threads and patterns that unite them and characterize the trend of thought that will lead toward a foreseeable future.

One example of such research is a 1991 study by Global Business Network that identified three broad scenarios for the global economy in the following twenty-five years: Market World, New Empires, and Global Incoherence.[5] The first trend emphasized the global economy and envisioned a further expansion of the multi-national corporations into Eastern Europe and the Muslim world. The second trend focused on the emergence of large economic blocs and their consolidation into political entities such as the European Union although similar developments for the Americas (NAFTA) and for the Pacific Rim (the Trans-Pacific Partnership) proved to be less advanced. The last trend took note of the phenomena of warlords and paramilitary organizations, and foresaw the growth of the drug trade and black markets.

Examining the implications for human beings is complementary to an investigation of the outward, visible signs of such trends of thought. The predictions made in this 1991 study have largely come to pass, though of course the article could not predict the specific events that would bring them about. From the perspective of 1991, Market World would require new inventions in the areas of electronics and computer science and the creation of a global work force capable of sustaining these advances in the realm of sub-earthly technology. More importantly, the success of this future trend depended upon consumers, human beings turning away from traditional culture, poetry, and the arts towards an electronic culture of music, movies, and messaging. The momentum of this trend crested as the home entertainment center moved into pockets and purses, and millions upon millions of people embraced a stream-of-consciousness life on social media enabled by devices created by an elaborate global network of suppliers and manufacturers that operated at a mammoth scale. The second trend, New Empires, needed patriots for its success. Human beings would also have to support the further development of sports and the cult of the body, which nurtured the authoritarian personality necessary to unfold a kind of super-patriotism that would willingly forego the protections of the Bill of Rights for the sake of law and order in society as a whole. The final trend, Global Chaos, would rely on developing a "gang" mentality that would serve the goal of spreading and deepening an illicit underworld that thrived outside the boundaries of any national or international law. According to the GBN study, this trend would not be cultural or political in its effect on the social organism, nor would it have an economic purpose other than its own survival. It pointed towards a human society without social norms holding it together, and the beginning of the end of Western civilization.

When the Wicked Witch saw that her Crows were dead, she blew her silver whistle three times. The Black Bees obeyed her command and swarmed to attack Dorothy. Again the Tin Woodman and the Scarecrow were awake and endeavored to defend her. The Scarecrow, victor over the Crows, took charge—as a good activist would—and ordered the Tin Woodman to protect Dorothy and Toto and the Cowardly Lion by scattering his straw over them so that they would remain hidden from the Bees. The Tin Woodman, victor over the Wolves, then stood up to face the Bees. He was proof against their stings, and the Black Bees, having broken off their stingers on his impervious shell, soon lay dead in heaps around him.

The Black Bees can be understood as a symbol of Market World, the modern trend that is most fully developed. The Bees, like the Wolves and Crows, are minions of the Wicked Witch, and their sting shows a kinship with their attacks. The deepening immersion of Americans in a culture of digital media and online entertainment, an educational system dominated by testing services, a health care system emphasizing surgery and drugs, and food services offering genetically-modified products grown with artificial fertilizers and pesticides constitutes not only a physical threat, but a soul one. The poison in the Bees' sting points to this danger.

Participants from across the cultural realm need to oppose these threats to culture. Ministers, priests, and rabbis need to enliven their congregations with a new theology of liberation and empowerment. Teachers need to inaugurate a new art of education and provide the home-schooling movement and the burgeoning alternative schools with a curriculum that fosters active thinking and returns testing to its proper role as a review technique. Similarly, doctors need to renew the medical field and create a health care system based on preventive measures and a holistic view of health care that employs natural remedies and homeopathic cures, making drugs and surgery a last resort. Culture in the traditional sense of the arts and literature also needs to be enlivened by artists who are not mere cameramen, but painters who capture the spirit of nature through a revival of neoclassic methods; musicians who are not technicians, but composers who weave the music of the spheres into new musical forms; and writers who are not simply arrangers of words, but poets and innovators who ennoble language to celebrate the human spirit. Ralph Waldo Emerson gestured towards such a new art of expression, saying that "new topics, new powers, a new spirit arise, which threaten to abolish all that was called poetry, in the melodious thunder of the new."[6] Poetry, Emerson declared, will lead in a new age. Walt Whitman, who consistently called for a new generation of poets to arise, connected the future powers of poetry with the very well being of the country:

> Of all nations the United States with veins full of poetical stuff most needs poets and will doubtless have the greatest and use them the greatest. Their Presidents shall not be their common referee so much as their poets shall. ... [The poet] is the equalizer of his age...lighting the study of man, the soul, immortality.[7]

The *buzzing* of the Bees indicates the nature of this third temptation of mankind that the Wicked Witch has unleashed. The sound of this buzzing pervades modern city life and has penetrated almost every corner of the globe. The machines of this present technological civilization contribute to it, but increasingly active are the advanced electronics that bought radio, cinema, and television into the twentieth century, the computer technology that united them into an information superhighway, and the digital technologies that have woven them into seamless networks. Contemporary thinkers frequently refer to the "hive-like" nature of the internet. Whereas Bolshevism threatened the will sphere of the social organism—the economic realm—and Nazism attacked the political realm, this new threat attacks the cultural sphere. It may seem strange that Dorothy and the Lion are so helpless against the Bees. In truth, most Americans do not see television, the computer, or the iPhone as a threat. Since when do entertainment and communication pose a danger comparable to that of Stalin and Hitler?

Baum showed the Lion and Dorothy being covered with the straw of the Scarecrow. He hinted at the role that thinking must play when confronted by the assaults of the modern media. The danger to the human being is not just that he is wasting valuable time, but that the feeling life (i.e. the Lion) is being hollowed out and that the ideals of the higher self (i.e. Dorothy) are being slain. Being a couch potato actually means being deprived of true feelings for other human beings and of access to those ideals that fire men's souls. Active, living thinking can confront the mindless entertainment and news of modern media and offer protection so that one's opinions can no longer be formed subliminally to coincide with the plan of some advertising executive or editorial board.

Almost a century after Transcendentalism ushered in the birth of American culture, the Roaring Twenties opened a window of opportunity for a broad cultural renewal. A powerful impulse in this direction lived especially in the African-American community, centered in the Harlem neighborhood of New York. Since the 1890s, the almost magical achievements of technology had captured the American imagination, especially those in light and sound. Along with the sound of New Orleans jazz appeared the talkies of the nascent movie industry. The application of technology to culture gave rise to radio and movies, and the first signs of American electronic culture appeared on the horizon. The new media introduced the popular worship of the movie star and sports hero. Europeans tend to have a more heightened sense for the evil embedded in American consumerism and often call it "Americanism." The effect of this influence on the culture of the 1920s was decisive. Perhaps the poem written in 1925 by one of America's foremost writers captured it best: "The Waste Land." So many talented and sensitive souls experienced the breakdown of cultural traditions and fled the country, as T.S. Eliot himself did, that they became known as "the Lost Generation." If these ex-patriots had remained in America and joined hands with the creative impulse arising in the black community, perhaps this enkindling of culture could have led to a broader rebirth and would be known today as something more than the Harlem Renaissance.

With the fall of Nazi Germany in 1945 and its subsequent partition, a nation released from the thrift of a wartime economy could begin building the suburban lifestyle—the initial or preparatory stage of Americanism. For the next few decades, the business of America became growth. Roads and interstate highways had to be built and cars manufactured to drive on them, malls had to be erected and stores stocked, TV and movies had to be watched and rock-n-roll listened to—all while consuming fast food. The success of the burgeoning American suburbs was only exceeded by the return on foreign investments spearheaded by the Marshall Plan. Denied access to the communist countries, multi-national corporations entered Europe and the Third World of under-developed countries. Their way often cleared by assassinations and clandestine missions of the U.S. Army, these businesses thrived as they grew to become international corporations. The U.S. military justified its support for capitalism over the rights of any democratic or progressive government by invoking the dangers of communism and the Cold War. President Eisenhower warned of the equivalent danger of the emerging military-industrial complex. The Vietnam War proved the veracity of his warning.

The Civil Rights Movement and the anti-war movement had their day, the Red threat rose and fell, and the military-industrial complex became the world's sole remaining superpower in 1989 with the fall of the Berlin Wall and the defeat of communism. This event opened the second stage of Americanism, which GBN named Market World: "the world converges into a single market. Trading barriers drop, and international trade skyrockets—the goods in shops become universal."[8] The 1990s saw the widespread adoption of personal computers, the creation of the home entertainment center, and the extension of the internet into the home with shopping online. NAFTA, GATT, and other free trade associations and agreements ignored workers' rights, created conditions for forced migration, and allowed drug cartels into the ensuing social vacuum. The Clinton years oversaw the expansion of Americanism into what had been the communist bloc in Europe as well as into China. When the dot com bubble finally burst in 2000 at the end of President Clinton's second term, the federal government actually had a balanced budget.

The danger of Americanism is that it tends to swallow up time, depriving a person of the opportunity to take in genuine culture. The Scarecrow certainly couldn't fight the Bees, but he could protect the Lion and Dorothy from their stings. He could hide the human soul and the higher self with the protective blanket of active thinking. This gesture of the Scarecrow and the symbol of the straw suggest the difference between actively reading an author's words by using one's imagination to convert word pictures on the page into mental images that become one's own, and passively experiencing moving pictures injected into the soul through the window of the eyes. It is the difference between reading Melville's masterpiece and seeing the movie of *Moby Dick*. The first gesture invites the cultural work into the soul, accepting it, recreating it, integrating it and making it personal. The second gesture observes a truncated surrogate at second hand and quickly moves on to the next experience—in effect, rejecting the cultural impulse. Rudolf Steiner pointed out that as man passes through succeeding cultural ages, he has a deeply rooted need to absorb the artistic achievements of the contemporary age. If a news station were to reject the art and literature of mainstream culture, for instance, and its listeners as a result refused to go to those plays or read those books, a consequence would follow. Such a person would impregnate his or her blood with a poisonous formative phantom—the venom of the sting—which could have been dissolved had the proper cultural impulse been absorbed: "This is the source of all the sicknesses of civilization, the cultural decadence, all the emptiness of soul, the states of hypochondria, the eccentricities, the dissatisfactions, the crankiness and so on, and also of all those instincts which attack culture, which are aggressive and antagonistic toward cultural impulses... The working of a poison is also always an aggressive instinct. In the languages of Central Europe this can be felt quite clearly: many dialects do not say that a person is angry but that he is poisonous." [9]

George W. Bush became the first President in sixty years to preside over a surprise attack on the American homeland. Two wars and two tax cuts after the destruction of the World Trade Center, he became the first President in eighty years to preside over a catastrophic stock market crash. The efficient cause of the housing market collapse that triggered the Great Recession of 2008 was the Bush administration's insistence on government deregulation, especially of the banks. Loose regulation means frequent crashes, which signal the doom of Market World. President Obama not only rescued the nation from the threat of a second depression, but acted to put in place safety regulations on the largest banks and businesses, as well as consumer protections that could help prevent such conditions from developing in the future. President Obama's successor, by contrast, has promised protectionism for American businesses and increased use of fossil fuels. During President Trump's first few months in office, deregulation rapidly accelerated through weekly executive orders that stripped constraints on businesses and markets, increasing the probability that further deregulation will follow and more crashes will ensue. Such policies are a clear sign of the end of the sway of the Black Bees as President Trump leads America in another direction.

# Chapter 11

## THE WINKIE ARMY
### AND THE U.S. ARMY

The sight of the Black Bees lying like little lumps of coal at the Tin Woodman's feet sent the Wicked Witch of the West into a towering rage. She could not use her silver whistle; it was now useless since the evil creatures it controlled had been defeated. She did, however, have slaves at her beck. She gave spears to the Winkies and ordered them to attack Dorothy and her companions. The roar of the Cowardly Lion sent the Winkie army packing. Nor were the Winkies hurt in any way, except by the Wicked Witch herself when she punished them for their failure.

The Winkies are like the Munchkins, the people of the East whom Dorothy liked very much. They are not inhuman spirits that seek to destroy human souls; rather, they are in thrall to the Witch and act out of fear. In Chapter Six, the Winkies were introduced as a symbol of the souls of people living in North America, and the United States in particular. Chapter Seven examined the deployment of the U.S. Army to invade Mexico in support of the Witch's second use of the Golden Cap. The treaty ending the Mexican War gave over one-half of Mexico's land to the United States, emboldening the Slave Power Conspiracy to expand the sway of slavery into those new territories. A civil war was necessary to defeat this effort. Chapter Eight showed the U.S. Army again playing an important role, even a decisive one, in support of the Witch's "socialist experiment" and in defeating Germany in World War I.

One unexplored aspect of the Wicked Witch's use of the U.S. Army in those wars was her penchant for "trigger events." Priming a country to send troops to fight a foreign war requires proper motivation. For the Wicked Witch, such motivation often entailed arranging an "attack" certain to upset and enrage the citizens of this land. Formulated as a slogan, such an event becomes a rallying cry that overrides reasonable attempts to find a peaceful solution. For the Mexican War it was "Remember the Alamo;" for World War I it was "Remember the Lusitania." To generate outrage sufficient to push the U.S. into World War II, a whole fleet had to be sunk at Pearl Harbor.

December seventh may be a day that will live in infamy, as Franklin Roosevelt declared after Pearl Harbor, but not for the reason he suggested. A generation before, President Theodore Roosevelt intervened at gunpoint—again with the U.S. Army—to create the country of Panama and complete the construction of the canal named after it, historical events that in truth must be seen as the necessary preparation for the United States to

fight and win a two-front war. Teddy Roosevelt's war with Colombia to shield the Panamanian separatists was based on the insight he had gained as Secretary of the Navy—that connecting the East and the West coasts of this country by sea was the key to victory. At the close of World War II, President Harry Truman's contribution to this hodgepodge of deceit was to unleash the atomic bomb against Japan. In doing so, he held the number of American casualties in the war below three hundred thousand soldiers by taking the lives of over one hundred thousand Japanese civilians and untold thousands more owing to the effects of radiation. Germany lost ten times the number of soldiers as the United States, while the USSR lost twenty-five times as many.

The goal of dividing Germany into two countries—a prerequisite for the advance of Americanism—was secured at Yalta in February of 1945 by Roosevelt, Churchill, and Stalin, three months before the war's end. The division of the world into two spheres of influence came about at Potsdam that July after victory had been achieved, this time with Truman in Roosevelt's seat. The ensuing Cold War raised the specter of "mutually assured destruction" (M.A.D.) between the two superpowers who would dominate the next four decades. In more practical terms, it led to the policy of containment, which sought to limit the spread of communism overseas, and the political use of the Red Scare and McCarthyism to suppress the labor movement at home in America. The Korean War began as a United Nations action in 1950 under its umbrella. General Eisenhower became President in 1953 with the expectation that he would contain the threat of Communist aggression, and he did so. When he left office in 1961, he gave warning that the military-industrial complex needed wars to justify its existence. Within only a few years, the U.S. had committed ground forces to Vietnam in a proxy war pitting the "democratic" south against the communist north. The Vietnam War attempted to fill the role of a patriotic war, but it lacked a trigger event to provide a visceral motive for revenge. The idea of containing communism north of the Demilitarized Zone soon narrowed to the hope that Ho Chi Minh could root out corruption in the southern capital that would soon bear his name. The draft and the loss of fifty thousand American soldiers fueled an anti-war movement that caused the war machine to rethink its policies and shift to a strategy of avoiding public scrutiny.

Nothing could prevent the final collapse of the Soviet Union. The Berlin Wall was torn down in 1989, and the Soviet satellites became nations again. Finally the socialist experiment was over, and Russia itself reemerged in 1991. Newly elected as President, George H.W. Bush announced the New World Order, and the U.S. Military was charged with its new role as the world's policeman. The first invasion of Iraq in 1991 was finished almost before it began; it lasted only 100 hours. Since the volunteer army seemed to suffer no casualties, the absence of a compelling trigger event did not cause a public relations disaster. When the Twin Towers fell a decade later, the former President's son, the second President Bush, decided that this trigger event not only provided a reason to invade Afghanistan, but that it also justified a second attack on Iraq.

The arguments advanced by the apologists for the minions of the Wicked Witch began with the writings of Marx and Lenin, whose critiques of capitalism failed to identify the problem correctly. If they had been honest thinkers, they might have identified the need for effective, socially progressive programs in pensions, health care, and education as the primary goal of government. The interference of the Western secret societies in the political sphere of the democratic republic is what needs to be opposed. With such an insight, they might have realized the ridiculous nature of a dictatorship of the proletariat as a means to promote the general welfare. Hitler's attempt to substitute Aryan supremacy and the eradication of the Jewish people is likewise a demonic alternative to the efforts of the Western secret societies to extol the genius of the English-speaking peoples and accelerate their leadership role in the present age, in particular at the expense of the democratic ideal of liberty and justice for all. What the Neoconservatives offered up with the Bush doctrine in 2002—the thin justification for waging war on a country that had not attacked us—was perpetual war. The backdrop of Orwell's novel *1984*, an endless land war in Asia, suddenly became a solution to the problem of popular support for the Bush II administration. The absurd idea of perpetual war is obviously worse than Western secret societies drumming up wars through the use of trigger events.

Relating the global nature of the attacks by the minions of the Wicked Witch to how their attacks manifested within the borders of the United States narrows the focus to how the three social classes of America actually responded to the threats that faced them. The domestic triumph over the Wolves (Bolshevism) through the victories of the labor movement in 1935 occurred much earlier than their global defeat with the downfall of the Soviet Union in 1991. The opposite happened with the threat of the Crows (Nazism), which were defeated in Germany in 1945, but were not overcome in this land until the passage of the Voting Rights Act in 1965 as a result of the activities of the Civil Rights movement. The Black Bees (Americanism) seemed to suffer a simultaneous defeat at the national and international levels since the Great Recession, which began in the United States in September of 2008, quickly spread throughout the world economy the following month. The downfall of the Winkie Army (the United States Army) was different than the other three. In Baum's tale, the Winkie Army is not destroyed outright, as are the Wolves, the Crows, and the Bees; they are simply sent packing by the Lion. Instead of an economic movement or a cultural movement, it took a political movement with a Bryan-like leader to roar its opposition to the use of American military force and send this minion of the Witch into full retreat.

In the 1960s, the Vietnam War provoked the formation of an anti-war movement. When the Democratic Party finally ran an anti-war candidate in 1972, George McGovern failed to inspire the further development of this movement and lost to Richard Nixon. The Watergate controversy diverted attention from the war. Following the withdrawal of United States forces in 1975, the Pentagon took steps to prevent the re-emergence of the anti-war movement, especially by eliminating the draft in favor of a volunteer army. Some forty years later, the Second Iraq War became another Vietnam, since it too lacked a trigger event. The Bush Doctrine and the trumped up intelligence about Saddam Hussein's weapons programs were simply no substitute. Neither did it help when President G.W. Bush celebrated "mission accomplished" just weeks after the invasion began. Not only did the casualties continue to mount, but the search for weapons of mass destruction—the ostensive reason for the invasion—floundered and ultimately failed. As the conflict dragged on year after year, the anti-war mood spread even into Republican circles. When the 2008 election cycle came into view, the Republicans ran a hero of the Vietnam War, John McCain, in the hope of maintaining their hold on the Presidency. The Democrats tended to ignore McCain and ran instead against President Bush. Candidate Barack Obama electrified his party with his message of hope and his inspiring speeches. In November of 2008, the Lion roared. A landslide of both the electoral and the popular vote carried the first African American into the Presidency. Just a month later, President Bush signed a status of forces agreement with the Iraqi government that began the long withdrawal of American troops.

  President Donald Trump can be viewed as a harbinger of a new direction in American politics, as the end of the last chapter suggested. His victories in the Republican primaries of 2016 amounted to a stunning defeat of the Bush policy of military intervention and nation-building. He ran against over a dozen opponents, including Jeb Bush, whose brother and father he frequently called out for their respective failures in the office of President. His triumph in the general election was equally a rejection of President Clinton's free trade agreements and candidate Clinton's vote in favor of invading Iraq. The Bush family and the Clinton family were the key proponents of New Empires and Market World. The flight of the Black Bees ended with the crash of 2008. Hilary Clinton's hope to revive them was no more likely to succeed than Jeb's would have been to win the longest war in the history of the United States.

## Chapter 12

# THE ATTACK OF THE WINGED MONKEYS
### AND Terrorism

---

The defeat of the Winkie Army made the Wicked Witch of the West stop and think, which means that she was considering an especially horrible and evil way to rid herself of Dorothy and her three companions. The Bolshevik Wolf had given up without a whimper with the emergence of the Russian Federation in 1991. The Nazi Crow cawed its last with Nelson Mandela's victory in 1994. The Black Bees of Americanism ceased their buzzing with the crash of 2008. Lastly, the Winkie Army began its long withdrawal in the following year. The Wicked Witch had one final power left—the charm of the Golden Cap.

Chapter Seven examined the Witch's first two uses of the Golden Cap. As Baum tells it, the Cap granted its owner the ability to call on the Winged Monkeys and make them carry out a task, but it could only be used three times by a single owner. The Wicked Witch had first used the Cap to enslave the Winkies and to raise herself into power, which brought about modern plantation slavery by means of the transatlantic slave trade. Her second use of the Cap enabled her to drive Oz out of the land of the West, which manifested as the Slave Power Conspiracy. By using the Cap a third time—with her Wolves and her Crows and her Bees dead, and her slaves ineffectual—the evil Witch would exhaust the magical powers by which she had perpetuated her rule. The fact that she decided to use it showed what a great danger to her Dorothy truly was.

The research of Global Business Network on the three major historical trends of the last quarter century named the third one Global Incoherence: "The world shifts into a free-for-all. Ethnic pride and tribalism explode. Nations impose selfish trading tariffs... Rinky-dink warlords become entrenched, and paramilitary organizations exert regional power. Nuclear blackmail surfaces... Black markets and very organized transnational crime flourish."[10] At the time these words were being written, Russia had just left the thrall of Bolshevism and was only beginning its move toward becoming the foremost country to exhibit this trend. Since that time, the former head of the KGB—the Soviet bureau for spies and assassins—has gradually amassed absolute power. Vladimir Putin's use of terrorism includes cyber-attacks, weaponizing the internet, and a global disinformation campaign meant to destabilize the West and disrupt the international order.

Political events in England in 2015 involving the victory of the United Kingdom Independence Party reflected this same trend. The UKIP opposed Market World by pledging to raise tariffs and also rejected New Empires by voting to leave the European Union. The leader of UKIP, Nigel Farage, even came to the United States to campaign for Donald Trump. Putin's influence on the American election of 2016 apparently included hacking the computers of Hilary Clinton and her campaign, slowly releasing damaging stories for months, and interfering with the computers used to tabulate results on Election Day. The Trump campaign already had on board a financial manager, Steven Mnuchin, who was a 1985 graduate of Yale College. He has since become the new Secretary of the Treasury and serves as Trump's financial connection to the Western secret societies. After the primaries began, the Trump campaign added a key strategist, Stephen Bannon. A major figure in the Alt-right, the man who coined the very term, the President's top adviser is not just a theorist or an apologist. Rather he is a go-between. He accompanied President Trump on his first foreign trip and visited the Vatican, where he met with the Pope's greatest opponent and critic, Cardinal Burke. Rudolf Steiner called the deal involving the secret societies of Catholicism (for example, the Jesuits) and of Freemasonry (for example, Skull and Bones) the conspiracy of the white and the black. A traditional view of Jesuitism and Freemasonry portrays them as mortal enemies, but the truth is much closer to the reality of the Cold War, which enabled the United States for decades to prop up the Soviet Union while bemoaning the Communist menace and enjoying complete economic reign in the "free world." A similar division of the world stands at the center of the deal of the white and black, which roughly cedes Catholic Europe and South America to the former, and England and Protestant Europe, and North America to the latter.

President Trump entered the stage of world history with all childish thinking and imp-like craziness of a Winged Monkey. His strong appeal to many people is based on his willingness to provide what in Roman times was called "bread and circuses." The gladiatorial contests in the Coliseum were more than just the entertainment provided by modern sporting events. They also possessed an element of bloodlust. The roundup of Christians in Ancient Rome enabled crowds of people to enjoy vicariously the torture and murder of human beings. President Trump's immigration policies have a comparable end in sight, to make a popular display of bringing pain and anguish to the millions who will be detained and whose families will be torn apart.

A deeper look at the terrorism that lies at the heart of Global Incoherence necessitates understanding it within an historical context. Terrorism is bound up with the activities of the Winged Monkeys. The inhumanity at work in modern plantation slavery as well as in the Slave Power Conspiracy of the nineteenth century characterize the horrors that accompany the appearances of the Winged Monkeys. The physical torture by slave-breakers, the murder of one in five captives by slave traders during the Middle Passage, and the rape and torture of slave women by their masters were only some of the atrocities visited upon slaves. Following the Hayes Compromise of 1876 and the advent of the Jim Crow segregation laws, the Ku Klux Klan unleashed the nightmare of cross burning, tar-and-feathering, and lynching.

Terrorism takes a further step into evil, however, if the obstacle opposing it is especially obstinate, street-wise, and kind-hearted. As an example, Steiner cites the efforts of the British Empire to gain control of China. When resistance emerged among the Chinese people at the beginning of the nineteenth century, Britain sent large quantities of opium to the areas of opposition. China finally ordered Britain to stop trafficking in the drug, which prompted the Empire to go to war, insisting on its right to free trade. The purpose behind the drug trade was to weaken a whole community's spiritual well-being and its ability to resist. The black communities in large American cities became similar targets in the 1960s. The presence of drug cartels and gangs is a clear sign of the activity of the Winged Monkeys. No foreign power made the United States accept huge shipments of opium and its derivatives, as the British Empire did to China. Rather, Big Pharma has made astronomical profits producing and selling opiates, while managing to avoid the legal jeopardy and punitive regulation that cigarette manufacturers were subject to in the 1990s. The American "war on drugs" has become an opiate epidemic reaching into all ethnic groups and classes of American society. Ironically, the name of the region in Indo-China that was the largest source of opium during the 1960s, and is second only to Afghanistan in the present day, is "the Golden Triangle."

The vicious attack of the Winged Monkeys is a picture of what is yet to come. It will leave the Tin Woodman dented and dashed upon the rocks, the Scarecrow shredded and stranded in a tree. The Witch will at last achieve the elusive victory she had sought through the other attacks of her minions. The defeat of the Tin Woodman and the Scarecrow suggest that not only industry and the working class, but even American culture and the professional classes will be devastated when terrorism appears in full strength on the shores of America. The end of American civilization and the collapse of the rule of law will leave the survivors—the Lion and Dorothy—with little hope of escaping their bondage to the Wicked Witch.

The victory of the Winged Monkeys is a prophecy that possesses a clear element of doom. Baum's vision may be compared to that of George Washington. One of the secrets of the Society of the Cincinnati, founded by Washington and his officers following the Revolutionary War, was revealed by Anthony Sherman and published in The National Tribune by Wesley Bradshaw in 1880.[11] Sherman related a narrative he claimed to have heard from Washington himself in the camp at Valley Forge in the winter of 1777. "Washington's Vision," as this secret is called, told of three great attacks on America. The first one was the invasion by Great Britain that General Washington and his officers were facing on that bleak winter night in Valley Forge. The second would come from within— the Civil War from which the Union would emerge victorious. The final test of the Republic would take the form of an assault upon America coming from all corners of the globe, an attack that would devastate the whole country. Melville's *Moby Dick* predicted a similar event, one that would destroy the American ship of state. Like Baum's prophecy, the visions of Washington and Melville held out hope that the ruin of the American civilization might yet lead to victory.

The chart on the following page summarizes the five attacks of the Wicked Witch on Dorothy and her companions.

| | PICTURE OF ENEMY (COMPANION WHO OPPOSES IT) | SPIRITUAL NATURE OF EVIL (IMPACT ON SOUL LIFE) | TREND IN WORLD EVENTS (SOCIO-ECONOMIC MOVEMENT WHICH OPPOSED IT) | HISTORIC DEFEAT IN AMERICA (PICTURE OF DEFEAT) | |
|---|---|---|---|---|---|
| 1ST ATTACK | WOLVES (TIN WOODMAN) | LOWER INSTINCTS (PASSIONS & DESIRES BECOME RUTHLESS WITH BLOODLUST) | BOLSHEVISM (LABOR MOVEMENT) | NATIONAL LABOR RELATIONS ACT (AXE CUTTING DOWN WOLVES) | |
| 2ND ATTACK | CROWS (SCARECROW) | EVIL MESSENGERS (THOUGHT LIFE BECOMES TWISTED BY RACISM) | NAZISM (CIVIL RIGHTS MOVEMENT) | VOTING RIGHTS ACT (TWISTING NECKS OF CROWS) | |
| 3RD ATTACK | BLACK BEES (SCARECROW + TIN WOODMAN) | MODERN TECHNOLOGY + CONSUMERISM (FEELING LIFE BECOMES HOLLOWED BY MATERIALISM) | AMERICANISM (ENVIRONMENTAL MOVEMENT) | THE GREAT RECESSION (SCATTERING STRAW + STINGERS BREAKING ON ARMOR) | MARKET WORLD |
| 4TH ATTACK | WINKIE ARMY (LION) | HUMAN SOUL LIFE (SENSE OF BEING ENSLAVED AND LIVING IN FEAR) | U.S. ARMY (ANTI-WAR MOVEMENT) | OBAMA'S FIRST ELECTION (LION'S ROAR) | NEW EMPIRES |
| 5TH ATTACK | WINGED MONKEYS | DEMONS (MADNESS) | TERRORISM (GRASSROOTS MOVEMENT FOR THE RIGHTS OF THE UNDOCUMENTED) | ??? | GLOBAL INCOHERENCE |

# Chapter 13

# THE IMPRISONMENT OF THE LION

## and the Grassroots Movement for the Rights of Undocumented Families

The instructions that the Wicked Witch gave to the Winged Monkeys differed from her previous attacks in one notable respect. Whereas previously she had commanded her minions to destroy all of the companions, she ordered the Monkey King to "go to the strangers who are within my land and destroy them all except the Lion." "Bring that beast to me," she said, "for I have a mind to harness him like a horse, and make him work." The consequent attack of the Winged Monkeys resulted in the destruction of the Tin Woodman and the Scarecrow; Dorothy and the Lion they brought to the Witch's castle for the Witch to do with them as she would. The Wicked Witch dared not attempt to harm Dorothy because of the kiss on her forehead, but she could certainly harm the Lion. To win over the Lion to do her bidding would be a great victory. By placing the Lion in a cage and starving him, the evil Witch expected to accomplish her purpose. The Lion, however, posed something of an enigma for the Witch. Whereas the Wolves and Crows represented evil transformations of willing and thinking that the Tin Woodman and the Scarecrow had respectively defeated, the attack that the Lion repulsed came from the Winkies, who were human beings. True, they were under the compulsion of fear, but the Winkies were not changed into an evil form and did not have to be killed. The Lion's roar sent them packing. The imprisonment and starvation of the Lion show the way that the Wicked Witch of the West hoped to achieve her objective of changing the feeling life of man into an evil form.

Dorothy defeated the Witch's plan by feeding the Lion some of her own food, which she smuggled into the Lion's cage during the night. The picture that Baum gives of Dorothy feeding the Lion is key to grasping the meaning of the evil Witch starving the Lion. Food itself needs to be understood spiritually. Man does not live by bread alone, but by the Word of God. Books contain sacred scriptures; they are the form that such living thoughts take on the earthly plane. Dorothy brought to the Lion that which truly sustained him.

Baum's tale pictures Dorothy holding long conversations with the Lion in these late night visits and cheering him up immensely. Such talks are opposite sides of the same coin, as it were. Conversations with the higher self (i.e. Dorothy) are certainly possible for those whose feeling life is open to them. The imprisonment of the Lion is a picture that goes beyond the negative effects that materialism has on the human soul, pictured by the buzzing Bees and Americanism. A kind of super-materialism will arise which will threaten to separate permanently the higher self of man from his feeling life. This occult imprisonment is not a poison, like the bee's sting, but a kind of negativity that traps human feelings as if in a cage and denies the life of feeling any access to inspiration.

Dorothy's life during the time of her captivity was drudgery. In effect, she was the Witch's slave. Unaware of the powerful charm of the Silver Shoes and oblivious to the meaning of the protective kiss she wore, she did not recognize her own power and was beset with fear. The Wicked Witch decided to take full advantage of Dorothy's naiveté, setting her to work about the castle. The Witch coveted the Silver Shoes and endeavored to steal them from the hapless girl. Unable to take them outright, the Witch devised a trick. She used an invisible iron bar to trip Dorothy, and grabbed one of the shoes when Dorothy lost it in her fall. The iron bar that trips Dorothy bears a similarity to the bars that restrain the Lion. The bars on the Lion's cage, solid and impregnable, picture how isolated the human being becomes in a reign of terror. The bar that trips Dorothy is, by contrast, invisible, a picture not of the outward face of fear, but of an inner one. Dorothy's fear is not like that of the Lion, who is called cowardly, though he is not. Dorothy, once trapped in the castle, is easily cowed by the Wicked Witch, afraid to confront her. Dorothy is tripped up by her own fear.

Looking at the Spirit of America's relation to the soul of the middle class more concretely helps to clarify the nature of the relationship between Dorothy and the Cowardly Lion. President Trump's plan for America expresses the grave danger that he sees facing this land. His proposed solution involves rounding up and detaining millions of undocumented people and breaking up millions of families. For two decades, the Mexican and Central American working class has experienced the nightmare created by NAFTA and the drug cartels, which entered into the vacuum created by the destruction of agricultural jobs as cheap American beans and corn flowed south across the newly opened border. They pray to the Lady of Guadalupe—the Spirit of the Americas, as the Pope officially named her in 2002—looking to her as the source of the strength and courage that they need in order to endure the threats of ICE agents, an unjust immigration law, a broken immigration system, and the reality of the bars of detention centers that separate them from their loved ones and friends. A comparison of the grassroots struggle for the rights of undocumented immigrants in America with the nonviolent movement for the independence of India, the Civil Rights movement in the South, and the anti-apartheid movement in South Africa would show that they are all cut from the same bolt of cloth. Columbia, the spirit of peace and brotherhood so closely united with America in the eighteenth and nineteenth centuries, became active in a new way in the twentieth century on three different continents. The narrative of America's fairy tale does not explore all of the ramifications of Columbia's activities around the globe, but focuses on events in this country.

## Chapter 14

# DOROTHY'S VICTORY
## and the Rebirth of American Culture

The plot of *The Wonderful Wizard of Oz* reaches its climax as, with one Silver Shoe in hand, the Wicked Witch becomes confident that she has finally won. When the Witch refuses to give back the shoe, she makes Dorothy angry—a fatal mistake. Dorothy throws the water from a nearby bucket onto her, causing the Witch to "melt away like brown sugar before her very eyes." The melting of the witch provides a picture of how her power ultimately will be dispelled. One thing that she cannot abide is water.

The climactic confrontation with the Witch can be viewed as prophecy, just as earlier events of the tale. The Wicked Witch's master plan included the attacks of the Wolves, the Crows, the Black Bees, the Winkie Army, and the Winged Monkeys. These singular events of the plot of *The Wonderful Wizard of Oz* have already appeared on the earthly plane of existence as the historical trends that can be called Bolshevism, Nazism, Market World, New Empires, and Global Incoherence. The social movement that will lead to Dorothy's future victory is also visible in earthly events at the present time, yet the immigration movement has not become the subject of intense media interest or academic debate. The minions who serve the Wicked Witch in earthly positions of authority see to it that the social movement for the rights of the undocumented, which is bound up with the secret of the water, is ignored, distorted, or hopelessly intellectualized.

The social movements associated with Dorothy's companions shed light upon the true nature of the struggle for immigration reform. The U.S. labor movement, the Civil Rights movement, the environmental movement, and the antiwar movement were not well-funded and extensively publicized, but rather they were composed of working class people and members of grassroots organizations. Undocumented immigrants have suffered from injustice and prejudice, have endured being ostracized and scapegoated, and are now in danger of being arrested in their own homes and imprisoned. In other parts of the world, gulags and concentration camps became the infamous symbols of the horrific rule of the hammer and sickle and the swastika. Under the Trump administration, undocumented immigrants in America face a danger of detention and deportation that is escalating daily, but this threat is simply an attempt to hide the true reason for what amounts to an attack on the entire Latino community. The grassroots organizing that has already taken root in Latino communities and molded them into a force sufficient to influence national elections belies the belief of the Western secret societies that the descendants of Romance language-speaking peoples are stragglers and must be ruled over by the Anglo-Saxon sub-race.

The Witch's attempt to steal the Silver Shoes from Dorothy, a failure that cost her dearly, shows how important they were to her. Having the charm of the Silver Shoes would have given her even greater power than both the Golden Cap and silver whistle combined. Only at the end of the tale does Dorothy learn of their power to carry her from the Land of Oz to Kansas and the earthly plane of existence. The power of the Silver Shoes to incarnate is what the Witch desires most, since her true goal is not to gain dominion for herself, but to prepare the way for the rulership of another. She is an emissary for one who has been called by different names at different times in various religions. In Dostoyevsky's masterpiece, *The Brothers Karamazov*, this great power of evil is called the Grand Inquisitor. The Witch's hope is to hurry the appearance of the Prince of Lies, who wants to be worshipped as the Prince of Peace. The Witch's obsession motivated her to try to take advantage of Dorothy's ignorance, the source of the fear that caused her to trip. The Witch's own ignorance of Dorothy's courage—the same bravery that inspired her to protect Toto when the Cowardly Lion attacked him—tripped her up as well. When the Wicked Witch refused to return what she had stolen and threatened to steal the other shoe as well, Dorothy had to act.

Baum's fairy tale contains within it the very water that the Wicked Witch so dreads. This water is related to the food and the conversations with Dorothy that so inspired and uplifted the Lion's spirit. It is restoration for the soul. Water is a picture of living thoughts, spirit knowledge that comes alive within the human soul. Water is a picture of the living stream of spiritual wisdom. The Witch can have nothing to do with such living thoughts and must keep them at a safe distance. In Baum's picture of the Witch, this means that she avoids going near the water at all costs. Human beings under her sway accomplish the same end by intellectualizing living thoughts. They adamantly refuse to enter into them and keep them at the greatest distance possible. The lack of such living thoughts can lead to the feeling of emptiness, a loss of purpose, and laments like those of T.S. Eliot in "The Hollow Men" and "The Waste Land." The presence of such thoughts brings insight and understanding. Writers who undertake the exercise of enfolding such wisdom into their essays and poems develop a sense for how it bursts the old forms of expression and demands new forms, demands even a new genre of literature. Emerson wrote about the author of this new type of literature in "The Transcendency of Poetry": "The Poet is representative—whole man, diamond-merchant, symbolizer, emancipator: in him the world projects a scribe's hand and writes the adequate genesis." "O yes, poets we shall have," he continued; "mythology, symbols, religion of our own. We too shall know how to take up all this industry and empire, this Western civilization into thought, as easily as men did when arts were few."[12] Whitman did the same in "By Blue Ontario's Shore," in which he heard the spirit of America, Columbia, calling for the Poet to arise. Only the Poet can satisfy the need of this country for a founding epic, for what is often called "the great American novel." Only the Poet can unite all of the millions of individuals in this land into a new American compact. This achievement will be the transcendency of poetry because it will reveal the secret of the water to be the capstone of American culture—a founding epic. Both Ralph Waldo Emerson and Walt Whitman hoped to assist the Poet by serving as his spirit guides.

Dorothy's victory presents a picture of how the rebuilding of America will occur following the great devastation of the Witch's rule. When the Wicked Witch melted away, Dorothy freed the Lion and told the Winkies the good news, asking for their help in finding and then reconstructing the Tin Woodman. The Winkies had tinsmiths aplenty for this purpose, and, finding Dorothy's dear friend battered and bent on the rocks, they lovingly mended and restored him. They even presented him with a gift—a new golden handle for his axe. Dorothy and the Winkies then searched for the Scarecrow. When the Scarecrow's empty clothes were found high up in a tree, the Tin Woodman put his new axe to good use and laid it low. Once he was carried back to the castle and stuffed with clean straw, the Scarecrow was again a new man. Reunited at last, Dorothy and her three companions rejoiced and spent many happy days together; yet they felt the need to return to the Emerald City and claim the rewards that the Great Oz had promised them. On the day that they were leaving, Dorothy went into the Yellow Castle where she had been staying and discovered the Golden Cap in the Witch's cupboard. It fit her as well as the Silver Shoes had once done, and she decided to take it with her.

The journey from the Country of the Winkies back to the Emerald City proved difficult indeed. There was no road from the Yellow Castle in the west to the Emerald City, so they became quite lost. Fortunately, Dorothy had the silver whistle. With it, she was able to call upon the Queen of the field mice for help. The Queen could not give Dorothy and her companions proper directions to take, but she did recognize the Golden Cap and knew of its powers. When the Queen of the field mice told Dorothy to look inside the Cap, Dorothy found the words of the magic charm that would activate its power. Reading them aloud enabled her to call up the Winged Monkeys, who, the companions discovered, would not harm them, for the strange beasts were bound to obey the wearer of the Cap. The King of the Winged Monkeys promptly acted on Dorothy's command to take her to the Emerald City.

There is great hope suffused throughout this picture of America's future—the rebuilding of the Tin Woodman, the restoring of the Scarecrow, the claiming of the Golden Cap and its power by Dorothy. These events lie in the future, so their meaning necessarily remains a mystery, though an illustration in this chapter helps clarify their import. The picture that Denslow drew of the Cap is identical to the cap that the sculptor Thomas Crawford had planned to use to adorn the statue "Freedom"— a sculpture of Columbia—that stands atop the Capitol Building. It is the liberty cap, also known as the Phrygian cap, which traces its symbolism back to ancient Rome and the cap given to slaves when they were freed. Crawford sculpted his model in 1855, when the tension between the slave states and the free states was reaching its crescendo, and just years before the outbreak of the Civil War. Jefferson Davis, then a United

*Left: The second version of "Freedom," sculpted by Thomas Crawford to crown the dome of the Capitol, 1855*
*Right: An illustration by Denslow of Dorothy in the Golden Cap, 1900*

States senator, became greatly incensed that the guiding spirit of America might wear the cap of Freedom, and he led his fellow Southern senators in a protest against it, demanding that Crawford model a new statue with the cap removed. Though he got his way then, he could not undo the prophecy that will finally bring it into Dorothy's possession.

Chapter Four discussed the first meeting of Dorothy and her friends with the Great Oz in relation to the theme of self-development and the personal meaning of Baum's fairy tale. That meeting now needs to be re-examined in the light of the prophetic meaning of Baum's tale and the world historic events that have unfolded. Her meeting with the Great Oz brought about a new mission for this folk soul or, using religious terminology, for this archangel. Archangels are emissaries or messengers of the Archai, often characterized as the *zeitgeist*, or the spirits of the age. By giving Dorothy the mission to kill the Wicked Witch of the West, the Great Oz took on the role of such an august spirit, showing himself to be one entrusted with the task of leading the spirits of the nations. When she and her companions return, triumphant, to the Emerald City, the Great Oz grants them an audience and bestows gifts of brains, courage, and a heart on the Scarecrow, the Lion, and the Woodman. But to fulfill his promise to help Dorothy return to Kansas, Oz has to think for many days. He finally concludes that the best solution is to cross the great desert surrounding the Land of Oz by air, and that in order to do so they must build a balloon to carry both himself and Dorothy. Yet when the balloon is finally built and filled with air, Dorothy cannot find Toto and chases after him. The ropes crack, and the balloon lifts away without her. Oz sails away in the air, to return to Kansas alone.

Baum's picture of the building of the balloon and its use in transporting Oz to Omaha may reinforce the insight into the deeper nature of the relation between Dorothy and the Great Oz. The balloon symbolizes the power belonging to the Wizard. It can be compared with the mythological picture of the talisman that gave Zeus-Jupiter authority over the Greco-Roman gods—the shield called the aegis. Dorothy's assistance in building the balloon points to the idea that she is to become a leader of nations, a Spirit of the Age. Rather than supplanting Oz and seizing his title, Dorothy is apparently to become co-regent. Understanding the two very different themes of *The Wonderful Wizard of Oz* as intertwined can help illuminate this concept of co-regency. The first theme, that of prophecy, presents future historical events as pictures and requires effort on the reader's part to live with these images in such a way that their deeper meaning may emerge. The second theme, that of self-development, presents the path that a person can take who would make the effort to learn the truth of genuine imaginations. The theme of prophecy points to outer events that will come to pass on the physical plane of history, while the theme of self-development describes inner steps of soul development that are necessary for any real hope of success in meeting those events. Dorothy can be viewed as the inspiring spirit of the outer social and political tasks that human beings will face in the future—and those that they face even now—while the Great Oz can be connected with the corresponding inner cultural and spiritual work.

The picture of the Great Oz returning to Omaha points to the opportunity for America to play a positive role in the near future, in an inner or esoteric sense. Baum's prophecy presents a picture of the near future in which this country experiences the Spirit of the Age working in an inward manner as the inspiring spirit of a cultural rebirth. Although the return of Oz to America appears in the form of a prophecy, it does have a precedent. The depth, originality, and vision of the Transcendentalists, which manifested the first full flowering of a uniquely American culture, attest to the fact that a Spirit of the Age was once directly active in this country. Oz's future activity will be different, however; the picture of Dorothy being left behind in Oz suggests that the guiding spirit of America will no longer be the medium for his activity, the intermediary for his pure intuitions. Another comparison with Greek mythology may further illuminate the imagination of Oz returning to Omaha. The god Apollo was said to be the god of truth and prophecy. He was even viewed as being directly active in Greek life, since from his oracle at Delphi he provided prophetic guidance to the kings and queens of the Greek city-states. Apollo was also active in the flowering of the arts in Ancient Greece. Through the nine Muses, his handmaidens, he inspired the great Greek artists and writers. The return of Oz to Omaha pictures the activity of the Spirit of the Age in American life, a renaissance that through his inspiration will lead to the flowering of a renewed American culture.

This renaissance will not belong exclusively to the cultural sphere, nor will it be simply a rebirth of Greek culture, a bringing over of old spiritual treasures into the present. It will transform the neoclassic impulse that was at work at the end of the nineteenth century in both the design of the White City for the Columbian Exposition and the renewal of the Washington Mall under Daniel Burnham's leadership. Oz's arrival in Omaha will signal a new form of art, an art that can transform even materialistic science and create the means to renew every aspect of modern life. This renewal has its source in the living thoughts that the Spirit of the Age will offer to human beings who are open to them, just as Oz presented such imaginations to Dorothy and her companions in the City of Emeralds.

That Dorothy will not return to Kansas as she and Oz had planned—that she will not travel in the balloon—shows that even after the defeat of the Wicked Witch who so threatens and seems to dominate the world at present, the time of America's leadership in the outer or esoteric sense will not yet have arrived. Dorothy's victory, however, will have an important effect. The restoration of the Tin Woodman, the resurrection of the Scarecrow, and the uncaging of the Lion point toward events of profound importance for the immense social and political problems that have beset America. In every area of modern life, individuals and groups have begun to work out of living thoughts to solve these problems and to create new social forms. The environmental movement is especially dear to the heart of the true Spirit of America. Insofar as human beings try to work out of a living picture of the earth—such as can be found in Thoreau's *Walden*—they will be granted insights and understanding from the book of nature. Their work will help to achieve the goal that constitutes Dorothy's third great mission, the one that she will take up after Oz's balloon floats away and she departs the Emerald City for a second time, to journey to the south and fully assume the mantle of the Spirit of the Americas.

# AFTERWORD

The climax of the plot of Baum's fairy tale occurs at the end of chapter twelve, the exact mid-point of *The Wizard of Oz*, with the melting of the Wicked Witch of the West. If the interpretation of Baum's modernized fairy tale presented in the preceding pages is correct, then this event is not only a marvelous creation meant to bring wonderment and joy, but a prophecy coming to fulfillment and close at hand. The next five to ten years will reveal whether this interpretation holds any water, as it were. For this reason an explanation of the source of this interpretation seems more pertinent than an attempt to pursue Dorothy's journey to the South and her meeting with Glinda the Good. For those readers who are interested in taking up such a study of the Spirit of the Americas, the map facing the title page may prove helpful.

The basis for interpreting Baum's tale as a prophecy for America came about due to a study group formed in May of 1985 in Chicago. Three members of the group who were present at the initial meeting continued to meet every three weeks for eighteen years. Magda Lissau, Kurt Nelson, and myself took up the task of researching fundamentalist sects, Eastern cults, and Western occult groups in a effort to characterize the spiritual background of this country. Some other participants joined and left. We were blessed to have had extraordinary mentors provide expert guidance, especially David Burbank from St. Louis and Rene Querido from Denver. Our research led us to uncover some amazingly positive and insightful individuals and the groups that formed around them, such as Edgar Cayce's Association for Research and Enlightenment.

On November 11, 1994, Kurt Nelson came to one of our meetings with a twenty-nine page, single-spaced proposal presenting certain insights that came to him much like Baum's had—as a bolt out of the blue. Magda and I read Kurt's interpretation of Baum's fairy tale with amazement. We immediately agreed to carry out the research that it entailed in the same manner as we had with Cayce and so many others. One of us would study the biography, another a major work, and the third the social movement, church, or organization that arose because of the author. By August 11, 1998 we had completed a one hundred and fifty page book, which we called *The Guiding Spirit of America*. It included a timeline that placed the crisis period of the Wicked Witch's dominion between the years 2020 and 2025.

In 2008, five years after our research group disbanded when Magda Lissau passed away, Kurt and I met again and shortened our draft of *The Guiding Spirit* considerably. The result was *Dorothy: a Prophecy and a Path for Americans*. The present book is a further condensation of that second draft. It includes historical events of the twenty years that had intervened since the 1998 draft and seemed to confirm much that we had predicted. What we did not anticipate was Dorothy taking on the leadership role of the grassroots movement for the rights of undocumented families.[13] The third mission of Dorothy as the Spirit of the Americas does strongly suggest that she would take on just such a mission. Once she inspired the Civil Rights Movement, and later helped to mitigate the stain of slavery on this land with the election of a black man as President. Surely now she should be able to help Americans atone for the great injustice done to Mexico, and, as the Lady of Guadalupe, inspire the undocumented to awaken the world-historic conscience and bring the evil of the fell Witch to an end.

# REFERENCES

A digital copy of the 1900 edition of *The Wonderful Wizard of Oz* is available online from the Library of Congress: http://www.read.gov/books/oz.html

1. Littlefield, Henry M. "The Wizard of Oz: Parable on Populism." American Quarterly, vol. 16, No. 1 (Spring, 1964), pp. 47-58. http://www.jstor.org/stable/2710826
2. Baum, Frank L. and W. W. Denslow. *The Wonderful Wizard of Oz*. Chicago: Geo. M. Hill Company, 1900, pp. 12-14. Available online from the Library of Congress: http://www.read.gov/books/oz.html
3. Steiner, Rudolf. *Theosophy*. Hudson, NY: Anthroposophic Press, 1994, p. 129.
4. "Jefferson's original 'Rough draught' of the Declaration of Independence." The Papers of Thomas Jefferson, Princeton University. Available online: http://jeffersonpapers.princeton.edu/selected-documents/jefferson's-"original-rough-draught"-declaration-independence
5. Garreau, Joel. "Conspiracy of Heretics." *Wired*, November 1994, pp. 98-106, 154-158.
6. Emerson, Ralph Waldo. "The Poet." Whicher and Spiller, ed. *The Early Lectures of Ralph Waldo Emerson*. Belknap Press, 1959. Vol. 3, p.363.
7. Whitman, Walt. *Leaves of Grass*. Library of America. New York: Literary Classics of the United States, Inc, 1982. p.8.
8. Garreau, *op. cit.*, p.100.
9. Steiner, Rudolf. *The Karma of Untruthfulness*. Forest Row: Rudolf Steiner Press, 2005. vol.2, p.5.
10. Garreau, *op. cit.*, p.98.
11. Anthony, Sherman. "Washington's Vision." *The National Tribune*, December 1, 1880, p.1. Available online from the Library of Congress: http://chroniclingamerica.loc.gov/lccn/sn82016187/1880-12-01/ed-1/seq-1/
12. Emerson, Ralph Waldo. "Transcendency of Poetry." *Natural History of the Intellect: the Last Lectures of Ralph Waldo Emerson*. Chicago: Wrightwood Press, pp. 92 and 95.
13. See Coleman, Walter L. *Elvira's Faith: the Struggle for the Rights of Undocumented Families*. Ann Arbor: Wrightwood Press, 2017.

www.ingramcontent.com/pod-product-compliance
Lightning Source LLC
Chambersburg PA
CBHW020657300426
44112CB00007B/420